# Struggle to the
# Top of the Mountain

ERNEST D. SIMELA, M.D.

authorHOUSE®

*AuthorHouse*™
*1663 Liberty Drive*
*Bloomington, IN 47403*
*www.authorhouse.com*
*Phone: 1-800-839-8640*

*Cover Photo by Nick of Patken Photographer, Inc. Lindenhurst, NY*

*Published by AuthorHouse  01/24/2014*

*ISBN: 978-1-4918-5908-7 (sc)*
*ISBN: 978-1-4918-5907-0 (hc)*
*ISBN: 978-1-4918-5906-3 (e)*

*Library of Congress Control Number: 2014901807*

# Dedication

This book is dedicated to my parents, Mayine Dick Simela and Makobo Elizabeth Mabhena, my wife Veronica Joseph Simela and my two sons Ashley Thabani Simela and Sipho Dubuya Simela.

# Acknowledgements

* * * * * *

I would like to thank the many wonderful people who helped me in the writing of this book. Some of them read the drafts and offered constructive criticism. I owe special thanks to my trusted and dedicated assistant Chariot Bermudez who typed the original manuscript. Finally my thanks go to the staff at Authorhouse and the editors at Chicago citation for their help and guidance.

# Contents

❀ ❀ ❀ ❀ ❀ ❀

# Introduction

※ ※ ※ ※ ※ ※

Sitting at the top of the mountain, looking at the winding trail down below, I now see all the obstacles that once were in my path and wonder how I made it up here. I believe the answer lies in a letter that I wrote to a pen pal in 1968. In that letter I wrote: "Where my intelligence fails me, my determination will carry me through." My determination to become a medical doctor was so strong that neither hell nor high water could stop me. I made the decision to become a doctor in 1957, when I was just thirteen years old. I had no idea how I was going to get there, and I knew that it was going to be a long struggle. However, I did not fully appreciate how difficult that struggle would be. I certainly had no idea how many obstacles I would have to overcome. This in itself was probably a blessing in disguise because I might have been discouraged if I had known that it would take me twenty years to reach the top of the mountain.

I might have been frustrated if I had known that it would take leaving my homeland and my family for twelve years without ever going back even to bury my father. I probably would have had a change of heart if I had known that Mr. Mitchell, a white student advisor at the University College of Rhodesia, would sit down and tell me with a straight face that I did not belong in the college. In the end, these obstacles only served to strengthen my resolve to climb the mountain and become a medical doctor.

No one in my family had ever attained that level of education, and indeed only a handful of my fellow black Africans had become doctors in the country at that time. The path was long and tortuous. I can see it clearly now from this mountaintop.

I recall those early days at Wanezi Mission, eating beans barely suspended in warm water day in and day out. I recall those days in boarding school when we kept dangerous farming tools in our dormitories because we worked in the fields half of the day and went to school the other half. We earned our keep, so to speak, much like migrant farm laborers do during harvest season. It was during those days that I decided I wanted to become a medical doctor. I did not know that I would do so many other things before I became a doctor. I found myself as a primary schoolteacher in 1964, a clerk in the housing department of the Bulawayo city council in 1966, a janitor in St. Paul, Minnesota, and a kidney dialysis technician in Minneapolis. All those were interesting experiences but not what I wanted to do for a living.

In 1968 the path would take me to a refugee camp in Francistown, Botswana. Three days in prison was not exactly what I had in mind as part of this long journey. It was an awful experience. I knew then that I never wanted to see the inside of another prison as long as I lived. Just when it seemed as if my dreams were going up in smoke and flames, I found myself in the United States, in Minnesota. With hardly a dollar to my name, in a foreign land, things looked pretty bleak to say the least. However, the inner strength instilled in me by my parents was there to see me through this one too.

I rummaged through several college bulletins and saw opportunities beyond my wildest dreams. I could not wait to grab them. But how? That was the question I asked myself. Ultimately, I did it the old-fashioned way: I went to work.

My first job, at Target, paid $1.40 per hour. I have been working ever since that time. The difference is that now I get paid a little more than $1.40 per hour.

I graduated from Hamline University in St. Paul, Minnesota, in 1973 with a bachelor's degree in biology and chemistry. I even achieved honors in biology. This was a huge accomplishment; I had achieved my first goal. It gave me the confidence that I could go on climbing to the top of the mountain. And I did.

In July of 1973 I enrolled at Albert Einstein College of Medicine in New York City. This was the most exciting and most critical moment in my struggle to the top of the mountain. My dream was turning into reality. I could see the flicker of light at the end of the tunnel. I was finally on the last leg of the journey toward being a medical doctor and I was not going to let go of this opportunity for anything.

It was hard. I was lonely. I had no money. My social life was on hold. But I knew what I needed to do. So there I sat in my dormitory room, barely six feet by ten feet. Day in and day out I told myself that I would get through this one too. Sure enough, four years later the moment of glory arrived. On June 2, 1977, I graduated from Albert Einstein College of Medicine with a degree, Doctor of Medicine. This was twenty years from the time that I had made the decision to be a medical doctor. I had finally made it. I had reached the top of the mountain.

I do not know how Sir Edmund Hillary felt when he reached the top of Mount Everest, but I know that I was thrilled. The joy I felt was beyond description.

## Chapter 1

# Early Childhood

* * * * * *

I was born in Zimbabwe, which was then known as Southern Rhodesia, on October 4, 1944. I was the fourth child in a family of eight children. There were two boys and one girl before me.

Life back then revolved around the family, the fields, the cattle, and just survival. The part of the country where I was born was called the Essexvalle district. Today it is called Esigodini. My family lived near Longfield School in the Nswazi reserve. Most of the areas were designated by the local school, and our local school was Longfield Primary.

My father had had the equivalent of about a sixth-grade education and training in bricklaying. He was a builder by trade, a construction worker. His primary trade was bricklaying, but that work included essentially the whole construction of a house, from the foundation to the roof, as well as doors, floors, and windows—everything. Most of the houses had no plumbing, so he was not too involved in the work of plumbing. Houses had no electricity, so there was no need for him to be an electrician. But the essentials of a house—walls, windows, and a roof—were his specialty.

My mother was a homemaker. She had a third-grade education. She was able to read and write my language, which is Ndebele.

Around the time that I was born, the whole Simela family was located in one little village. One member of the family had left to go back to South Africa, which is where we originally came from. He went back to look for a job and stayed there until he died. He lived and worked in Johannesburg. Otherwise, everybody else who bore the name Simela lived in one village.

About four years after I was born there was a program instituted by the government to put people in what was called *lines*. This was a restructuring of the areas where people lived in such a way that there would be roads and other services provided. People were moved around so that homes could be built along a somewhat straight line. My father had to move to conform to these regulations. The whole Simela family built their homes along one road.

Among the things that the family emphasized was the work ethic. Working in the fields was a top priority. As children, boys took care of cattle. That meant herding cattle, milking the cows, making sure that the cattle went to the dip tank to kill the ticks and that they did not get into other people's fields. They grazed in the pastures on communal land. Boys spent the whole day looking after the cattle, goats, sheep, and donkeys. In the evening they brought them back and made sure that they were securely placed in the cattle kraal, which consisted of a wooden fence and wooden gate.

Women attended to the most important part of life—providing food and shelter. They brought water from the wells or the river. They brought firewood from the forest. They made fire and cooked food. They brought the crops from the fields. Women probably did a lot more work than men. However, in our family everybody got involved in farming because my parents apparently recognized very early that this was the most important source of our income. It was the most important means for our survival. To pay for our education they had to grow crops and vegetables so that they could sell them. And so we spent a good deal of time in the fields.

In the summertime we cultivated the fields and, as the winter began, we harvested the crops and brought them home. But then instead of letting the land lay fallow over the winter months, we grew vegetables. In early fall, we also had vegetables ready to harvest and sell. In September or October, the planting season began again. The main crop was always corn. We worked all year round; it was the only way to survive.

My very early childhood consisted mostly of taking care of the cattle. At night the calves were separated from the cows. In the morning somebody would take the cows out to pasture. Little boys like me, preschool children, would take care of the calves around the house. Our job was to look after them to make sure they did not destroy anything. They didn't eat much grass, so there really was no need to take them out to pasture.

Around eleven o'clock or shortly before noon, we would put them back in the kraal just before their mothers came home. Then whoever was out in the pasture would bring the mothers home. We would milk the cows. Each calf was let out one at a time. It was allowed to suckle for a couple of minutes. Then one of us would milk the cow, after which the calves would suckle until they were content.

In the afternoon the cows went back to pasture. This was a daily routine. The little ones would stay home because if they went along they tended to fall asleep somewhere and get lost. So we tended to keep them home until they were strong enough to follow the rest of the herd. Only the older calves would go out to pasture for the afternoon with the rest of the cattle.

The same thing went for the goats, although we did not keep too many of them. But those who did keep goats would do the same thing. Donkeys were also an important part of this whole lifestyle. Many people used the donkey to plow the fields, or they would harness them to carry stuff around.

There were important tools and equipment that most families used. One of them was what was called a *sled*, which consisted of a large tree trunk with V-shaped branches cut into six- to eight-foot lengths. Smaller sticks were laid across the V. In holes drilled along the top of the V, sticks were placed vertically. This whole contraption was pulled by two or four oxen to carry firewood or crops from the fields. It was a rather destructive mechanism of transport because as the sled dragged along the roads, or along whatever route it created, it loosened the soil and caused major soil erosion when the rains came. Apart from the destruction of the trees, you also had the destruction of the land by soil erosion. However, it was a means of survival.

Those who were a little more advanced used ox wagons, pulled by either oxen or donkeys. The wagons had two wheels and were less destructive. However, not too many people could afford such a wagon.

There were many other work-related activities that people engaged in just to survive. Agriculture was the main means of survival. Subsistence farming, which consisted of tilling the land by hand or using the oxen and plow, was the one thing that everybody had to do. Crops, which generally included corn, peanuts, sorghum, rapoko, sweet potatoes, and a number of other lesser-known crops were planted by hand. Once the crops were above ground, we had to cultivate the soil to get rid of the weeds. They were tended to until they bore fruit, about two or three months into the season, and only then would we start to have corn to eat.

Initially com was eaten fresh from the field. Once it dried up, it was harvested, collected, stored in wooden storage shelters, and allowed to dry. During the winter months people shelled some of the corn and took it to the grinding mill to turn it into cornmeal.

This was used to make cornmeal porridge, the staple food in the country. It is made by boiling water. Cornmeal is added while stirring the pot until it produces a thick porridge, which is eaten with beef or chicken stew, vegetables, or other kinds of soup or milk. That's how people survived. The following season the same thing would happen all over again.

As time went by, people began to realize that they needed cash crops because they could not take the corn to school to pay school fees. People started to plant vegetables, cabbage, peas, beans, carrots, tomatoes, and sweet potatoes for sale. In the summer months they carried these crops on their heads, in buckets, or rode bicycles to the main road, which runs from Bulawayo to Johannesburg. Along that route people congregated at the bus terminal and train station to sell either fresh or boiled corn to travelers who would stop to buy something to eat. This would bring a couple of shillings or, on a good day, a pound.

Some of us collected our vegetables on weekends and put them on a bicycle and rode around the villages selling directly to the people in their villages. I did that for a good many years, on weekends and after school. It brought some money home—sufficient money to buy clothes, books and pencils, sugar, or bread.

In general the quality of life began to improve for many in the community. People were eating healthier meals with a decent mix of vegetables, meat, and starch. I did not start school until 1952 when I was almost eight years old. I learned how to ride a bicycle before I started school.

In 1950–51 my uncle Mabhena worked for my parents. He used to bring his bicycle. When he went to work, I would take his bicycle and try it one leg at a time, down the slope behind my house. I fell down many times. I did that a few times until I was able to hold the bicycle steady and eventually was able to get on it and ride down the hill. I used this skill later on in life when I rode the bicycle selling vegetables or delivering meat.

In January 1952, I started school at Longfield primary school. One of the reasons I had not started school when I was younger was that the school was quite a distance from home—about four to six miles away. My father did not think it was a very good idea for a little kid to walk that distance every morning and afternoon on an empty stomach. I was short—shorter than the average six- or seven-year-old child. In those days grass seemed much taller than now. No doubt it was because I was so short.

During the spring and early summer months the grass was wet from the morning dew. The small path that we took to school was essentially covered by the tall grass. By the time we got to school our clothes would be wet. For a little kid like me, running to school every day was a very challenging experience. It was still tough at the age of eight when I started school.

However, it was a very interesting experience. Fortunately, my mother always made sure that we had breakfast to eat. But there were many, many other children who went to school on an empty stomach.

A very loud bell rang at the beginning of the school day. If the bell rang before you got there, you had to run really fast; otherwise you would be punished for being late. The punishment was not very pleasant. You got a whipping. That was not one of my favorite things. I was always a little bit of a coward.

When the bell rang everybody would line up according to their classes. The teachers would take attendance and say prayers because the schools were run by the brethren in Christ Church. They were Christian schools. The beginning of the day consisted of singing a hymn and prayers. Then we would disperse into various classrooms.

There were not enough classrooms for the number of students attending. In my case, for example, in 1952 we attended class in the church, which was rather small, but it had to do. There were three different classes in that open church. One was Sub A, which was my class. There was Sub B which was the second class, located in the middle of the church and facing a different direction. And next to them at the pulpit there was the Standard 2 class, which faced in the same direction as Sub B. You can imagine three teachers, with anywhere from forty to fifty students, each trying to keep order within their own class and teaching in such a way that things made sense.

One teacher would be teaching the students how to write *a, b, c, d, e, f, g*. In Sub B, students were trying to do arithmetic: *2 + 3 + 4* and so on. At the other end of the room, you had the third teacher trying to teach the children how to spell complicated words like *listen* and *talking*. It was not an easy situation to say the least.

Somehow we all managed to pay attention to our own particular teacher. Now that I know something about attention deficit disorder and hyperactivity disorder, I can just imagine what would happen to a student with such a condition in this environment. They would go crazy and end up learning absolutely nothing.

My first experience in school was not very good. For the first couple of months (January and February, I believe), the teacher we had was tough on us. His name was Mike Tshalibe. He was extremely strict, and I thought he was not very pleasant to some of us. As a little child coming to school for the first time, I really did not like that.

I remember distinctly the times when we sat outside and practiced writing our ABCs. We did not have any pens or books to write in. So we lined up on the school yard on our knees and leveled the sand with our hands. Using little pebbles, we would write our ABCs in the dirt. The teacher would come behind us and look at the work that we had done. Anyone who did not do it right would be whacked on the back with a good-size stick. That did not go down very well with me. *I was terrified!*

Fortunately, right about the end of that first semester, Mrs. Simela, also known as NakaVeli, arrived to teach my class. Mr. Tshalibe, I believe, went to teach Sub B. Mrs. Simela was not soft in any way, but she was a conscientious and kind teacher. Although she was strict, she somehow was able to correct the students and keep order without instilling fear and anxiety in little children.

She did an excellent job. She laid down an excellent background for many of us. She certainly did so for me and for many people to whom I have spoken. She used a ridge, which had been erected in the school yard to prevent soil erosion, very effectively for disciplinary purposes. Whenever we were not doing the right thing she told us to go and lie down on this ridge. She would come around and whip us. You would lie down there on your belly and she would whip you on your back or buttocks. It was not a very pleasant thing. But we knew that whenever we were bad she was going to send us to the ridge. That was such a dreadful thing to have to do, but it kept us in line.

At the time of this writing Mrs. Simela has just retired after teaching for nearly half a century. God bless her.

That first year I did well in Sub A and went on to Sub B. By then I had already learned how to write a few things like *a-b-c,* and I believe I could write my name. At that time I certainly could memorize some verses from the Bible and did some mental arithmetic like 1×1 and 2 × 2. We did a lot of mental arithmetic. We would go outside the classroom and scatter all over the yard. We did not have papers, exercise books, or pens. We used a slate. There were special pens used to write on slate. The writing was erasable just like chalk.

And so with slate and pen in hand we listened to the teacher asking questions like 2 × 2 = ?, 3 + 3 = ? and so on. We wrote down the answers. When we finished, we exchanged slates. The teacher would read the answers and we graded each other's work. Once this was done you had only a few minutes to look at your work because you had to erase it and get ready for the next subject. The slate was an absolutely essential item in every student's life. Unfortunately they tended to break. When that happened it was often disastrous because most parents did not have the money to replace them. When the students lost the special pencil for slate, they would try to use a piece from a broken slate. But this usually scratched the surface and made it difficult to read.

This was a very poor way to learn. One could not take notes home for review, so it was important to pay attention in the classroom if you wanted to learn. There was no homework because we had no place to write it. This was probably a blessing in disguise for some students because they had nobody at home to help them with it. Some of us were lucky because we had brothers and sisters who were older and were in higher grades. In the evenings we gathered around a fire and went over the things that we had learned at school. Even though we did not have any notes or homework, these sessions were very helpful. They served as both a review and learning experience.

As if learning was not hard enough, the process of getting there and back was even worse. In the earlier grades, students went home around noon. This was not so bad except for those students who had not eaten any breakfast. As one progressed to the higher standards like Standard 1, 2, and 3, things got very rough. They did not serve any kind of food at school. Classes were dismissed at about 2:00 p.m. This meant that some students did not get home until three or four o'clock. That was almost a whole day without food.

However, nature always seems to know how to provide for those less fortunate. There were many different types of wild fruit along the way home. The children knew which ones were in season and where to find them.

As soon as we got home we changed our clothes. We had to keep the school uniforms clean. We would then get something to eat quickly and get ready for various chores. Most of the time there was work to be done in the fields. My father used to work at a farm called Mbalabala. He was the builder there. This place was five or six miles from my home. He used to ride his bicycle to and from there every day. So when we got home after school he was not there. However, my mother was always there to see to that all the chores were done.

One of my father's priorities was the welfare of the cattle. He always wanted to make sure that the cattle were taken care of. For that reason, during the weekdays there was always someone whose job was to take care of the cattle. Whoever was herding the cattle had to make sure that they took them to the best pastures. They were not allowed to mix with other herds, because bulls and oxen tend to fight. When that happened, sometimes they would scratch each other's skin. If my father saw any scratches, somebody would have to explain where they came from. And so, while herding cattle was generally a fun job, being outdoors, roaming free in open space, it carried with it a heavy responsibility.

Depending upon what the program for the day was, one of us would probably have to go to the pastures to trade places with the worker that was taking care of the cattle while we were at school. Sometimes we went straight to the fields or the garden depending upon the time of the year. There was always something to do after school. Sometimes we cultivated the crops by hand. At other times we watered the vegetables. And sometimes we just did maintenance work of one kind or another. There was no such thing as a free afternoon. On a good, light day our day ended at sunset. Otherwise we stopped working when we could not see what we were doing. During the plowing season things got even worse. Since my father was away all day, just like us, we got up very early, about three or four in the morning to go to the fields. We would work until about six o'clock. Then we would all go home, wash up, eat, and run to school while my father went to work.

In 1953, while my father was still working at Mbalabala, my parents bought a business! They bought a local butchery. This was a new challenge for my father. However, like everybody else, he was tired of working for other people, being treated like dirt, and paid very little. He knew that it was not going to be easy. However, it was an opportunity for him to work for himself and determine his own hours. This was important, because it would give him an opportunity to be home during the week to do the farming that he enjoyed. The business consisted of going out to the villages and cattle sales to buy cattle. He had to make sure that there was at least one cow to slaughter each day. The logistics of running this kind of business in the countryside was complicated.

The first problem was finding a place to keep the cattle that he bought and what to do with them before they were slaughtered. We did not have a farm to keep them on. The second problem was how to preserve the meat without any kind of refrigeration system. Electricity was virtually unheard of in the area where we lived. Amazingly, things seemed to fall into place once he got the hang of it. Virtually all the meat was sold by the end of the day. So there was no storage problem.

The meat was bought by local residents. However, there were some standing orders from such places as Mbalabala where he used to work, some boarding schools such as Mzinyathi Mission, and other places. Some people, such as teachers in the local schools, also had standing orders. The standing orders had to be delivered. I did that sometimes after school.

This business added a new and interesting dimension to our lives. We often traveled with our father to buy cattle from the villagers. Because of this, we got to know the area and the villagers rather well. They got to know us too. The business kept my father very busy, but he seemed to enjoy it very much.

The most important thing is that the business must have been profitable enough to enable my parents to educate all eight of us. They even bought a car in 1955–56. My father bought a big, light blue Ford pickup truck. It had a cap over the windscreen, which helped to keep the sun glare off. Inside it had a gearstick on the steering column, which was unusual. They called it the "champion gear." We all thought it was a beautiful thing and a great accomplishment for my parents.

Up until 1955 I had never ventured beyond a ten- to fifteen-mile radius from where I was born. The biggest obstacle had always been lack of transportation. Now that my parents had a truck, we were able to travel a little farther from home. My father was now able to take the fruits and vegetables directly to the big market in Bulawayo, the nearest big city. There they could get better prices for their products.

A great opportunity came along in 1955 when I was able to accompany him and his friend to the big city. We loaded up the truck the night before with crates of tomatoes and bags of cabbage. There may have been other vegetables too. Very early the next morning, and I mean very early, like two or three o'clock, we left home and drove all the way into town, about fifty miles. This was a trip of a lifetime for me. I was going to a place that more than 90 percent of the local population had never seen, and most likely would never see in their lifetime.

When we got there we picked out a well positioned set of tables in the center of the marketplace. There we laid out our produce attractively and waited for the market to open. All this was very interesting and new to me. It was even more exciting when the bidding started. The man in charge moved from table to table talking so fast that I did not understand a word he was saying. But somehow the buyers seemed to understand. The sellers simply collected the tickets and took them to the cashier to get their money.

Once we got our money, we went to a place near the market to buy breakfast. As we approached, I could see people inside sitting at the tables eating. But instead of going toward the door, we went around the corner to a window that had a sign over it which read Natives Here. *Natives* is what black African people were called. Through this window we ordered our breakfast. Tea was served in big tin containers. These were the cans that normally contain jam or canned fruit. Once they cut out the tops they used them to serve tea and coffee to the "natives." The bread was just chopped up into big chunks and served on a tin plate. And of course there was no table for us. So we sat down on the pavement and ate our breakfast.

This treatment was devastating to me. My father was the most respected man in the community, in my opinion. He was a successful businessman. But here he was treated like a tramp, like dirt. Such was my first experience in the Big City.

A few years later, I recalled this day when I joined the liberation movement in our struggle for independence.

My early childhood was not all work and school. There were many lighter moments and days of fun and games. There was a river about half a mile from my home. There, on both sides of the river, people had vegetable gardens. It was a beautiful place. There were birds' nests hanging from tall trees along the riverbank. Thousands of birds gathered every year. Birdsongs of all tunes and tones were heard all day long. Dozens of children gathered there after school and on weekends to swim, play and eat mulberries. There were dozens of mulberry trees planted along the river. By the end of the day everybody had dark purple hands, feet, and lips, and sometimes clothes too.

Some people played soccer using a ball made out of old clothes and rags. We could not afford to buy a real ball. Others enjoyed fishing using homemade fishhooks. Many more preferred swimming stark naked in the river. This is where I learned how to swim. This was genuine innocence of childhood and the pure unadulterated pleasure of childhood fun and games. It was priceless.

*Chapter 2*

# Pre-Teen Formative Years

* * * * * *

I call these the formative years because as I look back it was then that I made crucial decisions that have shaped my life. It was then that I decided that I wanted to be a doctor. It was also during that time that I learned about and understood the structure of our society. This was crucial in enabling me to find a place where I belong in society.

Even though I have not lived in the country of my birth for many years, I know where its greatest needs are. More importantly, I know how the chain of authority and power works. This has been crucial in establishing development projects in our region. During these years I learned about the politics of the country as it related to our people. I understood the suffering and the need for changes. So when I joined the liberation movement I knew exactly what the objectives needed to be.

Although the decision to stay an extra year at Longfield School was not strictly my own, it was an important one. It gave me a year to mature while I lived at home among my own family members. Otherwise, I would have been shipped to a boarding school somewhere. Because I was a year older, I had access to a lot of cultural events that children often do not get to see or do. For example, when a man comes to ask for a young lady's hand in marriage, children generally do not participate in the discussions. During 1957, my brothers and sisters were away in boarding school, and so I had the opportunity to entertain guests such as those who came to ask for my cousin's hand in marriage. It was quite an experience and a tremendous education.

Our culture was very rich but oftentimes very rigid. Fathers had the final word in virtually every issue that came up. The respect shown by the children and the wives was not out of fear but a tradition handed down from generation to generation. Men also showed respect for tradition. The kitchen was always a woman's territory. Men had very little say, if any, as to how this area of the house was run.

On the other hand, the cattle kraal was a man's world. There they did what they had to do. Very few women ventured there.

While all this structure was good for the orderly nature in which society functioned, it was often stifling. When the children ventured into the outside world, they often found it difficult to be aggressive in the presence of adults. In the structure of our liberation movements, this tradition of respect for elders came through loud and clear. Young people had great difficulty in voicing their opinions against an established leadership consisting of elderly men.

Up until 1957 Longfield School catered to children for only the first five years of school. After the first five years, children had to go somewhere else. Many went to boarding schools run by missionaries; others went to government schools in the city of Bulawayo. For a good number of others this was the end of their education.

Most of the time the reason for not going any further with their education was simply that there was no money. Going to boarding school was not cheap. The families paid tuition and board out of their own pockets. They paid for their books. But even before that, they had to pay for transportation.

My brothers and sisters went to Solusi Mission. This was an all-day journey. They traveled by bus from home to the city of Bulawayo. Even though this was only forty or fifty miles away, it took at least half a day. The cost of this travel was beyond what a lot of people could afford.

My home was in a typical rural area known as the *reserves*, or *reservations* in those days. Because of a lack of education, most people did not know what that meant. It was actually called Nswazi Special Native Reserve. To most people the word *special* implied *outstanding* or *different*.

It was different alright. Most people had at least five years of school. They were not starving to death because they had learned basic agricultural skills. Thus they were able to grow their own food. There were a few stores where people could buy basic things like tea, sugar, bread, and soft drinks. There were roads for the buses. People had been resettled in such a way that roads could be built through the villages. There were dams to hold water and halt soil erosion. Fields had been designed with ridges running through them to prevent soil erosion. There were health inspectors to teach people basic health skills such as hand washing and housekeeping to prevent diseases. They taught people how to build pit latrines for toilets to decrease the spread of disease through raw sewage.

This was indeed a special reserve because it provided industries with healthy, strong, young workers. These workers were also valuable because they understood instructions given in English. Those that worked in the gardens had already been taught gardening skills. Housekeepers had learned all about hand washing and basic hygiene. What more could an employer ask for?

We owe a great deal to the missionaries. Granted, there is a lot that they can and should be criticized for, but, on the whole, they did a tremendous job. Where I come from there was not a single government or public school. All the schools were built by the community and run by missionaries of various denominations. The most prominent denomination in our area was the Brethren in Christ church based in Harrisburg, Pennsylvania. Virtually all the schools that provided the first five years of education were run by the Brethren in Christ church.

They also had teacher training schools, which produced primary schoolteachers. It was the students from these schools that formed the core of the workforce—the reserve workers—that industries were looking for.

The mission schools had another influence. This was actually their main mission—to spread the gospel of Jesus Christ. They had a captive audience in the schoolchildren. They got them early, when their minds were open and still pretty much uncorrupted. They taught them how to read the Bible. The kids who could not yet read memorized a lot of Bible verses. The message was about the praise and worship of God. However, discipline was at the core of every lesson and activity. At the end of five years many students had been molded to join an obedient and disciplined workforce reserved for the growing industries in the cities.

Of course, not everyone ended up in the factories and urban kitchens and gardens. There were people like me who went a little further with their education. Some returned to Nswazi Special Native Area as teachers and other types of workers. Without those missionaries who gave us the fundamental education, it is hard to imagine where we would be. They certainly gave me a good start for the climb to the top of the mountain.

On the other hand, the education, laced with religion, obedience, and discipline, was superimposed on our culture, which was rooted in respect. It is hard to imagine how such a combination could produce radicals and dissenters. It was almost sinful to oppose the system. It was much harder to convince people that there was something wrong with the system than to make them follow the program.

Opposing the system meant not just defying the government but the church and culture as well. At least that is how it was perceived. The colonial government of the day understood this. They worked hard to keep the status quo. They gave the chiefs and elders the impression that they had unfettered authority. They gave the missionaries freedom to preach religion and educate the children. The two worked hand-in-glove to minimize any chance of dissent—be it religious, social or political. It is not surprising that the political leadership of our liberation movements did not come from the chiefs or religious leaders.

In 1957, Longfield School completed a block of classrooms. This enabled the school to add one more grade, Standard 4. Up until then, Standard 3 had been the highest grade. My class was the first Standard 4 class of students who did not have to go away to further our education. This had enormous implications for the students and the community. It meant that there were older children at home for various chores. They could help with their younger siblings. They were certainly going to be very helpful in the fields. Their presence at home would allow their parents to leave younger siblings in the house while they went out to the fields or did other chores.

For the students this was a year to mature under the protective wings of their parents. They could ask questions about our culture and traditions and get answers instantly from parents, uncles, and grandparents.

These young people would have opportunities to participate in traditional ceremonies such as *ukuthethela amadlozi* with a degree of understanding. This is a ceremony intended to honor, thank, and talk to ancestors. There are food, drinks, and dancing. Select elderly members of the family generally lead the activities according to tradition. It is a time to let the ancestors know what is happening to their children. It is also a time to ask for their guidance and protection. People generally sniff powdered tobacco. Some of the tobacco is shared with the ancestors by scattering it on the ground as one speaks to them. The same thing goes for beer. Some of it is poured on the ground before people start drinking. The music is traditional. Some people play drums. Others clap hands and dance in a circle.

Much of this tradition was becoming lost because children left home when they were still too young to understand. Thankfully, many others have kept their tradition, culture, and customs along with the Christian religion. One of the strongest criticisms against missionaries is that they encouraged people to abandon their culture and customs. They taught children that it was sinful to participate in these traditional ceremonies. As a result, when children returned from boarding schools with a little bit of education, they looked down upon those who practiced their cultural traditions.

Traditions such as memorial services to honor a deceased head of a family or an elderly person a year later were frowned upon by missionaries. Granted, the concept was a little different from that of Western cultures.

In Western cultures people hold ceremonies on the date an important figure died. The ceremonies generally commemorate the life and achievements of the deceased. In our culture the traditional ceremony took place a year after their death and was based on the concept that the deceased's soul was wandering around over the course of the year since they died. The ceremony was designed to bring the person home (*umbuyiso*). It was marked by song, dance, food, and praise. When all is said and done, this too is a celebration of the life and achievements of the deceased, just as in Western memorial services.

The year 1957 was a great one for me. I was twelve years old going on thirteen. As a part of Standard 4, it meant that we were not only the most senior students at the school, but in the whole area of Nswazi. No other school had a Standard 4. For all practical purposes we were the most educated people in the area. This made us feel very important. When one went to the local stores or wherever people from the community gathered, they recognized us. This recognition allowed us to take a peek into the adult world.

Generally in our society at that time children were to be seen but never heard. Children did not participate in many grown-up decisions that actually affected their lives enormously. The world of adults was a big secret never to be revealed to children. We were caught right on the edge between childhood and adulthood. Our educational standing gave us a little push toward adulthood.

Our teacher in Standard 4 was Mr. Douglas Mtshazo Nkala. He was the greatest. He was young, bright, friendly, dynamic, and very knowledgeable. He was just the right man for the job. I must point out here that Mr. Nkala was fresh out of high school. In those days the majority of teachers did not even have a high school education. High school graduates did not know anything about teaching methods, but they made up for it by having a high school diploma.

The fact that Mr. Nkala was so young was a great asset. We understood him better. He could relate to us better than the older teachers.

The country, and Africa in general, was going through difficult times. Like the civil rights movement in America, the movement for change in Africa was gaining strength. We did not understand much of what was going on. More importantly, we did not have access to information. We were thirsty for knowledge. We wanted to know about ourselves, our culture, our society, and the world. The standard curriculum did not provide this kind of information.

However, Mr. Nkala did everything to provide us with the opportunity to learn. He brought in people from outside the school to talk to us about a whole range of topics: from social affairs, culture, and tradition to politics. I remember a certain Mr. Maphosa, who was also a teacher. He spoke to us and used the word *enthusiasm*. This was a big word that we had never heard before. It was pretty exciting to hear everybody trying to use this big word afterward. This man had clearly triggered something in all of us.

There was a lot of activity among black people, especially in the towns. People were demanding equal treatment. They were calling for one man, one vote. But where we were, voting was a new concept. Black people did not vote in Zimbabwe at that time. The colonial government of the day responded to these calls for equal treatment by setting up what was called the *B-voter's roll*. We had no idea what that was. Mr. Nkala explained it to us. It was a voter registration system which allowed black people with certain qualifications to vote. However, their vote did not count as much as that of A-roll voters. The people who qualified for the A-roll were those who had a certain level of education or held some position in the community. There were differences of opinion about this offer.

Some black people thought that half a loaf was better than none. Others just saw it as an opportunity to get on the inside track. They enrolled. But the majority of people thought it was an insult to think that a black man's vote was less valuable than that of their white counterparts. To add insult to injury, black people had to qualify for this fraction of a vote. Any white person, even the homeless and the criminals, qualified to vote on the A-roll. Mr. Nkala helped us to understand all this.

It was at this time that Mr. Garfield Todd, then prime minister of the Federation of Rhodesia and Nyasaland, introduced the concept of *politics of partnership*. Mr. Nkala broke it down for us. Basically the idea was to gradually bring in black people to share in the governing process. By so doing, the black people, who until then had their own way of governing, would learn the Western ways. The hope was that in the long run there would be an equal sharing of power between black and white citizens. But that concept did not fly.

Neither the white constituency, nor the black majority embraced it. The whites thought Mr. Todd was selling out. The black majority thought that this did not go far enough. "One man, one vote" was the slogan of the day. Mr. Nkala not only made us understand the implications and details of this but our role in the society and politics of the land. This was crucial.

In 1957 I also learned a lot from my mentor, my sister Grace. It was the year when we planted sweet potatoes on flat ground rather than planting it on mounds of soil made into small ridges. When the time came to harvest the sweet potatoes we had a big and rough job in our hands. The soil was very dry. We needed picks and shovels. My sister spent all morning digging. When I came home from school, I would join her. It was also the year that she taught me how to wash dishes. One of us would wash while the other dried. A machine known as a dishwasher was unheard of. I think if one had bought a dishwasher, people would have come from miles away to see this miracle machine that could wash dishes.

My sister also taught me knitting. I learned how to make pretty cotton covers for food. These were useful in preventing flies from sitting on the food. They are also useful items to have when you go on picnics and have barbecues.

On many evenings my sister and I listened to music on a little box radio. It used a huge battery almost the size of a car battery. When the battery ran out, I would ride my father's bicycle six or seven miles to Mbalabala to buy a new one. This was our small window to the outside.

We listened to the BBC World News. I still listen to the BBC World News today. Since we did not have any television or newspapers, this was our only source for the news. It was the only way that we could follow the current events in the country and around the world. A lot of what I heard on the radio made sense because Mr. Nkala had given us the background at school. Between the BBC World News, my sister, and Mr. Nkala, I learned a lot about the world and politics.

My father was equally influenced by my interest in politics. Even though he was not what was called an activist, he followed political developments closely. One reason was that it was around this time that the African National Congress, a liberation movement, gained strength around the country. This movement was led by Mr. Joshua Mqabuko Nkomo, who had been my father's schoolmate at some point in time. He listened to the BBC News every night before he went to bed.

Interestingly, my father qualified for the B-voter's roll on the basis of his standing in the community. He was a businessman and had enough education to be a voter, according to the colonial authorities. However, he turned the opportunity down. To him it was tantamount to being a sellout.

The winds of political change were sweeping across Africa. The African National Congress was one more log on the fire to fuel this change. No one could have predicted that twenty-three years would go by before independence came to Zimbabwe.

My sister left home to go to nursing school at Mpilo Central Hospital in Bulawayo. We all missed her dearly but were all very happy for her. She had wanted to be a nurse, but there were few opportunities at the time. In fact, most people had to go to South Africa if they wanted to train as nurses. My father and I went to visit her a few months after she started. This was the first time in my life in a real hospital. I was very impressed by the cleanliness of the nurses. They wore white uniforms and white caps. Some of them had black capes over their shoulders. There were stripes and buttons on their shoulders. Of course I did not know what they meant. I was just bowled over by the whole picture. I could see myself working as a nurse. But there were no male nurses back then. There were male nurses' aides. But I did not want that.

The closest thing to being a nurse was to be a doctor. I made my decision then, in 1957, *and I never looked back.* I saw the mountain in front of me and decided I was going to climb to the top. Thus began my *struggle to the top of the mountain.*

When I went back to school I knew exactly why I wanted to continue with my education. I knew that it would mean many years of school. That did not bother me. I was going for it. This was a rather unusual decision to make, considering I did not know any black doctors. There were perhaps only two black doctors at that hospital. I did not know any of them. There were no professional role models to look up to except teachers, builders, carpenters, and other such workers. Even the preachers were generally not educated beyond Standard 6. We had no television or movies like *ER* or *Court TV,* which depicted doctors and lawyers. It is not surprising that many children dropped out of school after Standard 6. They had no incentive to go on with their education.

The whole country was abuzz with politics. Even people who did not know the English language knew about "one man, one vote." The highest ranking local politician, if one can call them that, was the chief (*induna*). At that time our chief was Mr. Makheyi Mabhena, who happened to be my uncle. The second highest office was his assistant.

These people had no physical offices except their home. Their powers were limited to prosecution of minor criminal trials and settlement of minor disputes. The court sessions were held on a rock outside my uncle's home.

The cases ranged anywhere from disputes over communal land distribution; a neighbor's cattle destroying someone else's crops; to someone hitting a drinking partner with a beer bottle, or other bad behavior at a beer party. Petty as all this may seem, the truth is it kept the fabric of the society intact. No man, regardless of how physically tough he may have been, wanted to be brought before the chief. There was unquestioned loyalty to the chief. Even the chief's assistant (*uimlisa*) enjoyed the same degree of respect.

Each village had its own immediate head (*usobhuku*). If there was a problem in the village, the village head was notified. If he could not resolve the matter, he reported it to the chief. (I say "he" because I never heard of a female *sobhuku*.)

This clearly delineated chain of command trickled down to the family. The wife and children obeyed the husband's every command. In return, society expected absolute responsibility from the man. He was not a man if he did not provide for the family. He was held responsible for the actions of all members of his family.

This multilevel but essentially standardized delineation of authority had some good elements. For children, every man and woman who was the same age as their parents was their parent. They had the right and authority to discipline the children if they were doing something wrong. As a result, children could not misbehave simply because their parents were not there. If they complained to their parents that someone had disciplined them, they would probably be disciplined again by the parents.

In 1957, the year I turned thirteen, I had many opportunities to see our area and to meet the villagers. My father used to take me along when he went to buy cattle for the butchery from villagers. Sometimes he went to check upon the cattle that he had loaned (*ukusisa*) some people who may have been in need. This was a practice that my parents had carried out for years. I always admired them very much for it. Some people needed a cow to get milk for their family but did not have money to buy one. Others needed an ox or two to use in plowing the fields. My parents would essentially loan these people whatever they needed. They could keep these animals for as long as they needed them as long as the animals were well kept. It was for that reason that we went around from time to time to see how these animals were doing.

Oftentimes they multiplied while at these people's homes. My father always kept track of what was going on. This gave me an opportunity not only to meet and talk to the villagers but to get to know their children as well. Some of these people were relatives that I would otherwise never have had the opportunity to meet. My father always introduced me and explained how we were related. I was able to understand and clarify for myself some of the intricacies of our immediate and extended family.

More importantly, I learned ways of dealing with people from my father. I witnessed firsthand the respect with which people treated him. I also saw how he treated them regardless of their age or station in life. It was always with respect.

I should point out here that there was, and perhaps still is, tremendous importance attached to one's last name. In my mind up until this point, any person who did not bear the name Simela was most likely not my brother or sister. They were more likely to be unrelated to me by blood or to be a distant relative. So I was a little puzzled when neighbors with such last names as Moyo or Ndlovu called my father *bhudi,* which means *brother.* In my mind this meant that their children were related to us. They were then traditionally my brothers and sisters. There was a little problem with this.

As a teenager I was beginning to be attracted to the opposite sex. I was not sure if these Ndlovu and Moyo girls were fair game. They were gorgeous. So I went to the source of true knowledge and wisdom, my grandmother. This was grandmother MaNcube Sodinda, my father's mother, who lived with us. She explained to me that there was actually no blood relationship between us and the Ndlovu or Moyo people who called my father their brother. However, they had been woven into the family fabric simply by living and growing up with our parents. Their grandparents had initially shared in the care of our grandparents' cattle. These people lived with the family. As they got older they raised their own families within the village and essentially became part of the family. This is why they considered my father their brother. This was a great relief. As for me and the girls in question, well that is history.

Grandma MaNcube was incredible. She was always a great influence and inspiration to all of us. She was independent to the end. Bless her soul. Granny cultivated her fields and garden by hand all day long. She always packed her lunch. She grew corn, peanuts, round nuts, and melons most of the time. She had about five acres of land. We helped her turn the soil and plant crops. But after that she took over and did everything herself. She even harvested the crops. We went there only to pick up the crops and take them home. Everything was done by hand in those days. Once the corn was dry, she shelled it herself by hand.

Most of the corn was used for cornmeal. So she would put some in half bags, which she filled only halfway so that they could be placed on a donkey's back and hang comfortably on either side. Granny had one favorite old donkey named Kopo. Once the bags were placed on Kopo's back she had no problem traveling to the grinding mill. There was only one grinding mill within a five- to ten-mile radius, located on a farm called Madlindevu, about four miles away. Granny walked all the way there and back.

The name *Madlindevu* was not a real name. But it became an institution. The real family name for the farmers who owned the grinding mill was Wright. However, the old man who ran the grinding mill had lost all his teeth. He grew a beard. Because he had no teeth he was always chewing. So people jokingly suggested that he was chewing his beard. The word *Madlindevu* means "the one who eats his beard." The name stuck.

The man died many years ago. But to this day the place is still called Madlindevu. Granny got along very well with that old Scottish man. My parents got to know the family very well. The daughter-in-law was very friendly. She used to visit our home and spend time with my mother. She spoke perfect Sindebele, our mother's tongue. Granny MaNcube was well into her eighties when she died in 1967.

The relationship between the Wright family, who were white, and my family, as well as with many other people in the community, always raises interesting questions about race relations in my mind. These white people lived with and among Black Africans for many years. They learned the language and culture of the people very well. They related to the community very well. Is it possible that if the rest of the country had learned to relate to each other as we did with the Wrights, there would not have been racial tensions that tore us apart?

Mrs. Wright was so free and so familiar with African traditions that she could actually teach some of us a thing or two. I remember seeing her with my mother in the kitchen, showing her the easiest way to make cottage cheese. We had been doing this for generations. But Mrs. Wright had developed a way that made it easy to make large quantities using the same containers. Can't we all just get along?

My parents did something else over the years which I admired very much. They took in many disadvantaged children from friends, relatives, and perfect strangers and raised them along with their own. I do not know the stories behind each and every child. All I know is that there were a lot of children who grew up with us. Some of them were related to us, but many were not. My parents treated them and educated them exactly the same way as they treated us. When they bought clothes they bought them the same clothes. At Christmas time we shared the same beach ball, which was our standard gift. What they did was akin to the foster care system in this country, except that they did not get paid for it. All these children grew up and went on with their lives elsewhere.

I was, however, very touched by one incident in recent years. My mother died in 1991. In 1992 we held a memorial service for her at home, the very home where she had cared for all these children. As I was ushering people into the living room I turned to look at a well-dressed gentleman walking behind me. I suddenly recognized him as Mr. Jamela Mathuthu. We had not seen each other in about forty years. Jamela and his two brothers had lived with us for many years. They were not related to us in anyway. I was impressed that after all those years he felt it in his heart to come and pay his respect to someone who had given him a healthy start in life. My parents had given him an opportunity to get an education and a shot at being a productive citizen. He apparently took the challenge and opportunity and made excellent use of it. Jamal was by then a successful businessman.

It is not that my parents had that much more to give other people in material terms. But they had big hearts. They lived with an attitude of gratitude. They were always willing to give more than they received. And I admired that.

I have revisited the pre-teen years of my life many times in my own head. The first and last years of my time at Longfield School always come to mind. The first year is because of the confidence and desire to learn instilled by Mrs. Naka Veli Simela. Fortunately, the first teacher that I had for a couple of months in Sub A was replaced by Mrs. Simela. I doubt very much if he would have inspired me and given me the appetite for further education. I was downright scared of and discouraged by him.

But Mrs. Simela came to my rescue. I sincerely believe that she gave me a very strong foundation. Even though she did not say it in those words, she made us feel the sky was the limit. I believe that it was this confidence in her students that helped me to persevere through many difficult patches along the way to the top of the mountain.

Mrs. Simela has given about half a century of her life to the education of young children. Teaching was a profession that she loved. Whenever she was in the classroom she gave one hundred percent. This total dedication came through loud and clear. That is why her students were also inspired to give one hundred percent to learn whatever she was teaching. Mrs. Simela has recently retired from teaching. I and many others are grateful for the role she played in our lives.

My last year at Longfield School is important because it is the year in which I left my hometown. Since 1957, I have not lived there again for longer than one month at a time. But is also the year when I learned a great deal about a whole range of subjects. At home I had learned about my family tree and my culture and tradition more than at any other time. At school, of course, there was Mr. Douglas Nkala. He opened my eyes to the history, politics, and much more about the society in which we lived. For the first time we understood the role of colonialism. We understood our place and role in the politics of the day. Mr. Nkala went on to practice what he preached. He joined the liberation movement and suffered a great deal in the course of fighting for the independence of Zimbabwe.

Unfortunately he has since died. But I will always treasure the lessons that he taught me. As for me, 1957 was a great year. I turned thirteen years old. I was ready to leave the nest and go to boarding school.

*Chapter 3*

# Wanezi Mission
# 1958–1959

⁂

I finally had to go to boarding school in January 1958. There was no school nearby that offered Standard 5. Unlike my brothers and sister who had gone to Solusi Mission, I went to Wanezi Mission. Solusi Mission was run by the Seventh Day Adventist Church, which was the church to which my mother belonged. Wanezi Mission, on the other hand, was run by the Brethren in Christ Church, the same denomination that ran my primary school. This was a major break with tradition. It probably affected my life enormously. I have never been able to evaluate its impact. However, I do know that I have never belonged to any particular denomination because of this break with tradition. I have always been religious. But I have never been baptized in any church.

Wanezi Mission had a reputation for being a tough but good school. Many before me had survived it. I was sure that I could too. I had already made a commitment in my mind to stay in school until I became a medical doctor. It was generally believed that being a doctor was hard. People believed that doctors had to read a lot of big books. I believed that too. And so Wanezi was just fine by me, because it had a reputation for being a good school.

The whole idea of traveling by bus to a faraway place was exciting. When you put this in the context of the times it is easy to understand why. There were very few cars at Nswazi. There were also very few buses. In fact, there was one bus that passed through our area. It was a red-colored bus called Imbizo. Very few people had ever traveled by bus; they had no reason to. The lifestyles of many people consisted of subsistence farming. As long as a family had a few cows that gave them milk and a couple of oxen with which to plow the fields, they were set. They bought clothes from the local store perhaps once or twice a year. Their needs were met by local vendors. So a journey of fifty miles by bus was a major event to prepare for and certainly was something to be excited about.

While I was excited about the prospects of going to Wanezi, there was also an element of fear associated with it. Wanezi Mission was an all-boys school. It was not known for gentle treatment. First of all, the idea of being away from home for three months at a time created a certain level of anxiety. It was hard to imagine not eating Mama's cooking for three months.

As if that was not bad enough, Wanezi had a bad tradition of hazing newcomers. This often consisted of rough treatment, including beatings. Sometimes fistfights broke out. This was every newcomer's nightmare. Fortunately we had older fellow students to protect us. To this day I cannot find any good reason for this tradition. I have not been able to find its origin to explain it to me.

The taunting and teasing started at the bus stop. This would go on for several weeks into the school year. For those of us who were not used to rough treatment, it was pure torture. Even so, we did the same thing to the newcomers in the following year. Thankfully, I personally did not experience any beatings.

This whole tradition of hazing had interesting results. People bonded tightly according to where they came from. It only made sense that you hung out with those who protected you. By the time one developed friendships outside of that circle, the homeboy bonds were sealed.

There was another tradition which was strong at Wanezi. Other schools had it too, but at Wanezi it was institutionalized. That was the tradition of *idale*. In the society at large, *Idale* was a place where people, particularly men, gathered to discuss matters of the community. At Wanezi this was a place where people from various communities gathered to share stories or just shoot the breeze.

The school was located on a huge piece of property, so there was plenty of space. People from different parts of the country or various communities staked out a spot away from the dormitories. This may have been a place under a big tree which provided shade or a place with a large rock where people could sit. Whatever the reason may have been, it was the place where people with common interests gathered.

*Idale* served a variety of purposes. It was a place where people made a fire to keep warm in the winter. They made a fire to boil water, roast corn, or just sit around and chat. They got to know each other. Sometimes students even found out that they were related to each other when they talked about their families. Early in the term they shared food they had brought from home. It was also a place where students helped each other with schoolwork. And it was sometimes a library where students sat down to study.

On weekends it was a great place to kill time with friends or just to listen to wild stories and tall tales. This was the place where students came to share good times and bad times. Sometimes there was a coalescence of various smaller groups into a larger one based upon mutual interests and understanding. It was a place where students sometimes just broke into music and dance. Other groups would start singing and others would come to join in and dance.

The student accommodations consisted of several camp style dormitories. They were all one-story grass-thatched buildings. There were generally two larger rooms with one small one in the middle. The larger rooms accommodated ten to twelve students. The smaller room in the middle was reserved for the prefects. Prefects were responsible for law and order. All the rooms had nothing but bare walls and a cement floor. There were no beds, no wardrobes and no bathrooms. There was absolutely nothing in them. There was no running water. No pictures on the walls.

The outside yard was kept free of grass. The main reason for this was to deter snakes from coming into the rooms. This is true of most homes in the countryside. The idea is that the snakes will not want to go across an unprotected patch where there is no grass. Generally snakes do not move very fast on dirt. This was very important because we slept on the floor. The last thing that I wanted to have happen was to wake up with a snake next to me.

The students were expected to bring their own blankets, pillows, and a straw mat to put on the floor. Those that were sophisticated enough to know about towels brought them. Otherwise a T-shirt or any piece of cloth was good enough for drying oneself after washing. There was no hot water.

*Idale* came in handy in the winter because one could make a fire and warm up some water. Otherwise cold water, a bucket, and soap were all that was available. There were no showers or bathtubs. The toilets were pit latrines located behind the dormitories. There were no lights in the toilets. Unfortunately, most students could not afford to buy flashlights either. One could only pray that they did not have diarrhea during the night.

Residents of each room staked out a space on the floor where they would sleep. Every night we spread the straw mat on the floor on top of which a blanket was placed. A second blanket would be used for a cover. I never saw any student with sheets. Every morning we picked up our bedding, folded it, and put it up in a neat pile in the corner somewhere. There were a few instances where students wet their blankets at night. This was a big problem because it was embarrassing for them to have to take their blankets outside to dry. And of course, no one wanted to sleep next to them. In the summer, when it was too hot to sleep in the rooms, we slept outside—as long as it was not raining.

I guess the snakes and other crawly creatures were afraid to come near such a big crowd. I wonder what our hair looked like after sleeping out on the ground on a windy night. But it was fun. It was like camping all year long.

The assignment of rooms was somewhat voluntary. As a result, people from the same area of the country tended to stay together. This was good because it created a very peaceful atmosphere in the dormitories, which was absolutely essential in an all-male student school. It was all the more important because we kept dangerous weapons with us. Every student was given an axe, a hoe, and a sickle to use during working hours. If there had been any disturbance in the dormitories, these items could have caused serious harm. It would have been a disaster. But no such disturbances ever occurred.

The school enforced a strict code of conduct. The prefects had a lot of authority. They could give students demerits for just about any infraction. A demerit meant punishment over the weekend. Of course, severe infractions could even result in expulsion. All in all there was an incredible spirit of comradeship among students. Some of the long-lasting friendships built then have survived to this day.

Wanezi Mission is located in a remote part of the country in the Filabusi district. It is about twelve miles south of the main road to Greater Zimbabwe (Zimbabwe Ruins). The closest store was the one at the junction between the main road and the road to Wanezi. Even this store was just a small country shop where one could buy sugar, bread, and soft drinks but very little else. However, it served as a drop-off point for our mail. There was a bus that brought mail for the school from Bulawayo in a bag. A messenger was then sent from the school to pick up the incoming mail and drop off outgoing mail. Occasionally we asked the messenger to buy us some bread and sugar. If there was enough money, we bought tea leaves as well.

On the weekend we would then have a feast at our *idale*. The bread tasted so good that we ate it slowly all afternoon. But sometimes we bought the bread to make a little bit of money. You see, if we bought a whole loaf of bread, we could slice it into many pieces and sell those for more money. People bought the slices at breakfast time and put them in their porridge. With a little extra money we could buy more for our feast. What a way to earn a living!

One might wonder why these other students did not buy their own loaf of bread. The truth is that we sold our slices for three pennies. That may have been the only money they had for the term.

Life on this farm school was strict. There was law and order. There were boundaries beyond which one did not dare stray. Getting caught outside the boundaries was a severe infraction of school rules. The punishment was severe. It could even result in expulsion from the school. This is why we could not even go to the store ourselves. Even though we had the time on Saturdays and Sundays and it was only twelve miles away, we were never given permission to walk there. It never happened.

There were old mines near the school. Those, too, were off limits. Obviously they did not want students to go there because they might have found beer and liquor to drink. Then Reverend Hershey would have had some real problems on his hands. Even worse than that, the students might have found girls at the mines. That was a no-no.

We were required to speak English from Monday morning to Friday night. If one was heard by the prefect speaking any other language during this time he would get a demerit. That person would be punished over the weekend. This was actually a useful rule because it forced everybody to learn a foreign language. English was not only the means of communication at school, it was the official language of the country. By encouraging students to learn English, the school actually enhanced the students' career opportunities. English was also the language used in all industries.

The driving force behind the school administration was the principal. When I was there, the principal was Reverend Hershey. He was from Messiah College in Harrisburg, Pennsylvania, where the headquarters of the Brethren in Christ mission was located. Reverend Hershey was a heavy and stocky but incredibly energetic gentleman. He drove an old jeep that did not seem to need a road. This thing was able to climb mountains and cross rivers. The principal was seen just about everywhere in his jeep.

He seemed to have his eyes on everything in the school. The only place where we did not see much of him was in the classrooms. I suppose he knew that the teachers had everything under control there. His main concern was to maintain law and order. And that he did well.

Despite the keen eye of the principal, some students managed to do naughty things. One of the most common infractions was the students stealing maize from the fields. They would get the maize and go into the wooded area of the farm near the mountains. There they made a fire and roasted the corn or boiled it. But Reverend Hershey was a smart man. He would go to an open field from where he could survey most of the farm. From that vantage point he would see smoke coming from the valley or the mountains. Then he would drive his infamous jeep to a point close to the site and leave it there. From there he would walk.

Invariably he caught the students red-handed. The old workers on the farm called him Mjumbu Uyatshelela, believed to be a term for a slippery and virtually invisible animal. Reverend Hershey was incredible.

There was a home craft school located on the premises, but far from where the boys lived. The students at the Home Craft School were mature women. They seemed old to me at the time. But at the time I was only thirteen years old. Some of those people could have been my mother; some of the students in my class and the senior class were much older than me.

Even the toughest rules and regulations could not prevent the raging hormones from getting some men and women together. Students were frequently caught on the wrong side of the boundaries with women from the Home Craft School. The punishment was generally severe. In some cases it resulted in expulsion from the school altogether. But more often than not the punishment involved digging trees and clearing more land for cornfields. This was a rough and tough job.

Reverend Hershey would go to the farm and pick out the biggest trees. He would mark anywhere from ten to twenty of them for the student to dig up and cut down from the roots. The student was not allowed to ask for help. This could take days or even weeks because the soil was generally hard. It was a hard red clay soil with lots of rocks. But that did not seem to deter some people. Each year several students were caught in the act. I suppose where there is love there is a way.

When Reverend Hershey was not growling at the stubborn boys, he was a sweet teddy bear of a man. I had the opportunity to ride around on a tractor with him during the plowing season. He was also a good preacher. When he was on the pulpit in his clerical garb, you would never believe that he was the same rough and tough man on the jeep. He took whatever he did seriously, and preaching the gospel was his main mission. His wife was always kind. She was rarely seen anywhere else besides their house, the church, and the orchard.

Occasionally on Saturdays we were assigned to take care of the orchard. On one Saturday, we had to carry manure and leaves using wheelbarrows. We saw what looked like gigantic oranges. They were just too good to resist. On our way out of the orchard we grabbed some and threw them into the wheelbarrow. Then we covered them with leaves. Just as we walked through the orchard the friendly Mrs. Hershey stopped by and started chatting with us. I think my heart skipped several beats when I saw her. But thankfully she did not seem to notice anything in the wheelbarrow. When we got way out of her sight we stopped to eat our spoils. We were so disappointed that we almost cried. We had picked grapefruits instead of oranges. The things were so bitter we could not eat them. If we had been caught we would have been punished for stealing something that we had not even been able to eat.

Alcoholic beverages and smoking were strictly forbidden. These were not only forbidden as part of school rules but on religious grounds as well. To consume either one was considered a sinful act. In retrospect, this was a healthy thing. Many people who smoke generally pick up the habit in their early teenage years. This was the age group that we were in. This one regulation probably saved many lives from the hazards of smoking. We had no access to any beverages, including Coca Cola, let alone alcoholic beverages. The only kind of alcoholic drink that people would have had access to was home=brewed corn meal beer. But since all the villages were out of bounds, that too was not available.

In order to get a beer one would have to break at least two rules: one for being out of bounds, and the other for drinking alcohol. It is likely that they would have cut class or some other activity as well. All these infractions would most likely result in expulsion from school.

Life in the school revolved around education, religion, and work. Working on the farm was a large part of our daily activities. We grew corn and beans, which were our staple diet. We also grew some vegetables like cabbage, onions, and carrots. We occasionally had some of these vegetables thrown into our meals. For the most part our meals were the worst. We ate cornmeal porridge every single morning. There was no tea or coffee. There were no eggs or bread. There was no juice of any kind. Our lunch consisted of cornmeal and beans suspended in warm water. I lost a lot of weight the first term at Wanezi; I could not stand the sight of those beans.

Dinner was more of the same cornmeal porridge and beans. At some point in time I had to eat this stuff otherwise I would have starved to death. I got used to it. I actually gained weight and grew a few inches over the two years I was at the school.

Cattle were kept on the farm. One cow was slaughtered on Thursday, so on that day we got meat for dinner. An interesting aspect of this is that there was a student by the name of Mission who had to be present when the cow was killed. I did not understand this at the beginning.

I found out later that there was a certain ritual that went along with killing a cow; otherwise some people would not eat the meat. It turned out that this gentleman was from the Lemba tribe. These people do not eat pork, rabbit, hare, and scaleless fish. This is exactly what is written in the book of Leviticus, chapter 11 of the Old Testament. When preparing meat for consumption, the animal is killed in a *kosher* manner by bleeding. The Islamic custom is comparable to this practice.

Over the years researchers have established a DNA match between the Lemba people and the people of the Hadramaut region of the Yemen Republic, which was once part of the Sabuean Empire. Most surprising of all was the discovery that members of the most senior Lemba clan carried the Cohen Modal Haplotype gene, which is a distinctive feature of the Jewish priesthood. This genetic pattern is carried by the Y chromosome, according to the researchers. It is significant because it means it is passed on from generation to generation through the male line. Every Thursday we ate that meat and did not know that we were eating kosher meat.

I venture to say that 99.9 percent of us did not even know the word *kosher*, let alone what it meant. But it is good to know that the school cared enough to observe its students' ethnic customs and traditions.

The remote farm environment belied the competitive academic nature of this school. There were just two grades. They were known as Standard 5 and 6. This is the equivalent of about seventh and eighth grades in the US. Each grade was divided into two sections: 5A and 5B, and 6A and 6B. We had four great teachers.

Mr. Maphendla Moyo was the headmaster. He was an experienced teacher with an excellent ear for the English language. He was not only an excellent teacher but also a good speaker. He was a great interpreter who was even tapped to translate for the Reverend Billy Graham when he visited the city of Bulawayo. He had the stature of not just a teacher but of a father figure as well. Everybody gave him the respect he deserved. Mr. Moyo taught Standard 6.

Mr. Ndirnande was a tall, clean gentleman who was always very well dressed. Even the dust from the chalkboard seemed not to get his clothes dirty. Mr. Ndirnande wore eyeglasses. So some students called him Mr. Glasses. One must understand that very few people wore glasses in those days. Even those who needed them went without them either because they were never examined or could not afford them. That is why Mr. Ndirnande stood out—simply because he *wore* glasses.

He was a no-nonsense teacher, dedicated to his job of teaching Standard 5. He gave his students his undivided attention and demanded the same of them. In addition, he was a good musician and led the music in church.

Two young dynamos completed the team. Mr. Vita Tshuma was young, dynamic, vibrant, easygoing, and always pleasant. He taught Standard 6. His classes were always exciting. He made learning fun. They *had* to keep classes interesting. Otherwise students might fall asleep after working hard in the fields.

The weather was generally warm and there was no air conditioning. There were not even fans in the classrooms. Worst of all, sometimes the students attended afternoon classes after eating a heavy meal. Mr. Tshuma kept the students awake whether they wanted to be or not.

Finally, there was the one and only Mr. Daniel Njini Moyo, an excellent teacher. There was no room for a long face in his classroom. He was lively, funny, and always on the ball. He mixed everyday social life with his lessons so well that a day in his class went by quickly. However, at the end of the day he made sure that you had learned something. Mr. Moyo was also in charge of soccer. I guess that's why he always had his eye on the ball.

I got to know the latter two teachers very well. They were both bachelors who lived in the bachelors' quarters near our dormitories. Mr. Njini Moyo's brother, Khalayi Njini Moyo, was a student in my class. Khalayi and I became friends, and we were classmates together for many years thereafter, until we attended the University of Rhodesia.

On weekends we used to cook for the two teachers whenever they were at school. The fringe benefit of this was that we got to eat rice and a decent beef stew with properly cooked vegetables.

Wanezi was a religious school, so of course the most important subject was religion. One of the missionaries taught religion to both grades. Most of the religious teaching was done in church. We had morning prayers every day. On Sundays there was Sunday school, which was not just a service but an instructional session. Then the rest of the day was dedicated to Sunday services. People from the community attended as well. There were people who worked in the school and lived within walking distance. They all worshiped in the school church.

There were very few other denominations in this part of the world, and so most people belonged to the Brethren in Christ Church. The combination of intense religious teaching and tough rules and regulations helped to keep the boys in line.

There was a tremendous amount of competition between the sections in each grade. The teachers probably felt this, too. They pushed their sections to do well. They themselves worked very hard to prove that they were the best teachers. And so they gave their students everything they had in their bag of teaching tools. There was not much to offer by way of teaching aides. There were a limited number of books to read. There were no bookstores around. Even if there had been bookstores, the students would probably not have been able to afford to buy books. There were no transparencies, no slides, and no videos, and this all happened long before the days of computers. The teachers did not have many learning tools or study guides to give students so instead had to motivate them to study hard. The students picked up on this energy from the teachers and engaged themselves in serious academic competition among each other.

There was not much to distract anyone from their books except the hard manual work, but even this soon became part of the daily routine. When we were not in the classroom, chances were we would be at work in the fields or gardens, or busy clearing new fields for more corn and beans. There was no television to watch. We had no radios or Walkmans to listen to. There were no girls to distract our attention, though perhaps the older students had problems with women at the Home Craft School. And so the bulk of our energy was concentrated on reading.

Skill courses were taught outside of the regular curriculum. These included carpentry, bricklaying, and gardening. The grades obtained in these courses did not count much toward the academic grades. As a result, they did not consume much time. There was not much to study, but I actually enjoyed the bricklaying course, which was taught by Mr. Mchimba. This may have had something to do with the fact that it was my father's trade. I had been exposed to it in my childhood. I knew all about the different sizes of bricks. I knew about the different kinds of bonds: the simple bond, the double wall bond, and the herringbone bond. I had watched my father build many houses. I did well in the course. We actually put our skills to work building a house for one of the teachers on the school premises.

The school was poorly equipped as an academic institution. Many of the things that we take for granted in today's schools were nonexistent or in very limited supply. There was no library to speak of. The books that were available were outdated or irrelevant to our needs. There were very few extra books to read. There were no movies to watch for entertainment or for academic purposes. Considering that there was no cinema within our borders or anywhere near the school, this was not surprising. In fact, this was a subject that did not even come up in any discussion about the needs of the students.

Many of us knew nothing about movies. If we had seen a movie it was because one had come to our area once or twice much the same way that a circus comes to town. There were no newspapers or magazines to read. Once in a while one of our teachers or missionaries might bring an old magazine or newspaper for the class to read a particular article. Regular subscriptions to magazines were unheard of. The only things that we had for reading were the textbooks for the various subjects such as English, history, Ndebele, geography, arithmetic, and the Bible.

One of the best and most valuable activities was the Friday night debates. This was the time for everyone to show off their command of the English language. Too bad there were no girls to impress.

A topic was selected in advance. This gave the opposing sides time to prepare their points of view. But more importantly, those who took part had time to learn new phrases. They looked up new expressions and big words (known as jawbreakers) with which to impress the judges and critiques. As a result, one of the most popular books that was purchased and carried around by students was entitled *The Student's Companion*. This book contained English words and phrases along with their definitions. The most important part of the book was the examples it gave of how these words and phrases are used. This book was much like a thesaurus. Students pored over this book and tried to find expressions and words they had never heard before. Oftentimes a word sounded unusual only because no one knew the correct pronunciation.

The debates were generally lively but orderly. There was always a teacher in the audience to keep order. And of course, the prefects were always there, ready to give demerits to anyone who got out of line. If one had made it to Friday night without a demerit, they did not want to jeopardize their weekend with any silly mistakes.

There was a tremendous amount of pressure on those of us who were considered the best students. We were expected to know virtually all the words and phrases used during the debate. We were often selected to be the critics. A critic's job was to write down all the grammatical errors made by those debating. At the end of the debate, the critic would correct those mistakes for the benefit of the whole group. Sometimes this created another debate, because there was no agreement on the correct usage of a word or phrase. Fortunately, the teacher in the audience had the final say.

This was a great learning experience. We learned not only how to speak English correctly, but how to speak in public. We learned how to think and express ourselves on our feet. It is not surprising that many of us expressed a desire to be schoolteachers or preachers. It is unfortunate that we did not have role models for lawyers and parliamentarians. I daresay many of us did not even know then what a lawyer or parliamentarian did. We had never seen one. We did not have any TV programs like *ER* or *Law and* Order. There was no TV at all.

The Friday night debates were a great way to cap the week. Remember that we were not allowed to speak any other language but English from Monday morning to Friday night. This was a good time and place to practice what we had learned during the week.

The true battleground was in our academic performance. Our grades were the ultimate measure of our performance. The cumulative score when all the numerical grades were added determined one's position in the class. There was a position given for each section. Then there was a position determined when the two sections were combined. This was the big one.

Of course, being number one was the position we all strived to achieve. Obviously, the teacher's pride and prestige were enhanced when his students did well. The students battled each other not only to be the best as individuals, but to beat the other section as well. I was in Standard 6B. My toughest competitor was Mr. Dennis Nzama, who was in 6A. He managed to beat me all year long when we were in Standard 5. He continued to outdistance me during the first and second terms of Standard 6. I just could not get a handle on this guy.

I thought I studied as hard as, if not harder than he did. He always managed to beat me by a few points. However, when the finals came I was determined to come out on top. I gave my studies every ounce of energy I had. On the last day of school we all gathered in the church to get our results. It was nerve-racking to sit there and wait while the teachers dotted the i's and crossed all the t's. We both knew we had done well. The question was who was going to take number one. I was thrilled when my name was announced. I was right at the top of the class. I had finally edged out the legendary Dennis Nzama to put my Standard 6B on top.

Dennis was extremely disappointed. He even cried as we left the church. But that was the competitive nature of the students at Wanezi Mission. Dennis and I had been friends, and we continued to be friends even after those results.

We all left the school to go our separate ways in December 1959. This was the Christmas holiday season. Schools were closed until the end of January. It was a time when most students went home to their families and friends. Many children like me celebrated their success in school and looked forward to another year. Others were not so lucky; there was no automatic advancement to the next grade. If you did not do well, you had to repeat the grade. I know classmates who repeated the same grade two and three times.

There was no summer school. For those who had not passed, the holidays were miserable. They knew that they had to go back and do the same thing all over again. They had just flushed twelve months of their lives down the drain so to speak. But this was not the end of the world.

In fact for the Christians, it was the beginning. They celebrated the birth of Jesus. Even the non-believers celebrated the holiday season by getting together with family and friends. They usually slaughtered a goat, cow, or chicken and cooked lots of food. This was the one time in the course of a year that most people were off from work or school. It was a time to relax and reflect upon the events of the past year.

Many of my fellow students and families had big decisions to make at the end of the year. They had to decide what to do next. Many of us went on to Matopo Secondary School to continue with our academic studies. That was an easy decision.

Others went to Mtshabeizi Teacher Training School to train as teachers for primary school. In today's society, seventh-grade graduates do not go into teacher training. But they did then. They generally did a pretty good job of teaching.

Some people went to trade schools to pursue careers in carpentry, farming, and construction. Many of the other trades, like electrical technology, plumbing, and mechanical engineering were not taught in African schools. For many other students Standard 6 was the end of their education for a variety of reasons. Some had no money to continue with their studies. They had to go to work to support themselves and the rest of the family. Unfortunately, my friend Dennis was one of those disadvantaged children. Perhaps it is thoughts about people like Dennis that have inspired me and my wife to form a scholarship program to help able but disadvantaged children. Our scholarship program is designed to help these students by paying their tuition and other educational expenses. We will never know what a brilliant student like Dennis might have contributed toward the development of the country.

There is no doubt that there were students who simply did not have the encouragement to continue with their education. They were lured by the bright lights of the cities and so went to work in the factories and other industries. I know some people who joined the army. Whatever our final destination was to be, in general, the two years at Wanezi Mission were a great experience.

My life was changed forever. I knew that I had what it would take to eventually achieve my goal of becoming a doctor. It seemed as if all I needed to do was to continue to work hard and keep my focus on the top of the mountain. I had no idea how many obstacles lay ahead of me. But I knew I was going to get there someday.

An interesting development occurred at about this time. My father had worked for many years at Mbalabala (Balla Balla), a farm owned by the Sanderson family. Within the farm there was a business center that included a train station, a bus stop, a post office, a general store, a bakery, and a liquor store. Just before I graduated from Wanezi Mission, a secondary school for white students was built on the farm. The name of the school was St. Stevens. My father and Mr. Sanderson thought it would be an interesting idea for me to go to that school since I had done so well at Wanezi.

But of course, deep down they both knew there was no way that the racist farmers would let a black child into their school. Racism was rampant. The struggle for independence was raging all across Africa. Zimbabwe was no different.

My application to the school would have been a challenge to the status quo. There were just too many forces against the idea for it to even get off the ground. So I went to Matopo Secondary, an all-black student school to continue my education.

*Chapter 4*

# Matopo Secondary School 1960–1964

❋  ❋  ❋  ❋  ❋  ❋

After two years in an academically demanding boarding school like Wanezi Mission, the transition to Matopo secondary was easy. All the fear and anxiety associated with being away from home were gone. I also knew, from talking to other people, Matopo was a better school. The students did not beat up on the newcomers as they did at Wanezi. Besides, I was a big boy now, almost sixteen years old.

Buoyed by the excellent record that I had achieved at Wanezi, I felt a true sense of accomplishment in going on to secondary school. There were not many people from Longfield or Nswazi that had ever gone to secondary school. Many of my classmates were not coming for various reasons. Some had not been accepted into secondary school. But most did not have the money.

My parents had a lot to be proud of. In a place where very few children went beyond Standard 6 (about eighth grade), my parents were now sending their third child to secondary school. My sister and one of my brothers had gone to Solusi Mission for their secondary education, or JC (junior certificate) as that grade level was called. Once again I was breaking with the tradition. Instead of going to Solusi, I was going to Matopo. My oldest brother had gone through teacher training at an SDA school, which was an equally impressive accomplishment.

By now my family had mastered the routine of preparing for boarding school. After all, they had done it for more than five years for four children. We each got a big black metal trunk. This was for our clothes, books, and whatever else we needed. Generally, the trunk was too small to fit clothes, blankets and books. So the blankets and a straw mat were wrapped around the trunk and the whole thing tied with belts. There was almost an art to this ritual. I had done this for two years while attending Wanezi Mission.

At Wanezi Mission we slept on the floor. There were no beds or mattresses. Therefore, we had to have straw mats. Every night you spread the mat on the floor and then your blankets on top and slept between two blankets.

Matopo was a secondary school. It had a little more class. Each student had a small bed, so I no longer needed a straw mat. However, the trunk was still standard equipment. Blankets were required since the school did not provide them.

The second most important item was a smaller metal trunk for storing food. Remember, we were going away for about three months. There was no such thing as a weekend pass. Parents rarely visited the school; it was an expensive and long journey. Very few parents had cars to drive to the school—perhaps one or two. So we packed some dried foods such as roasted peanuts, dried beef, and dried sugar cane. Some people carried wild fruit such as *xakuxaku*, which may have been boiled and then dried. This way one could keep it for a long time. We also carried some freshly cooked food such as sweet potatoes and boiled peanuts, if they were in season. Boiled corn was also another favorite.

One reason students carried a variety of these foods was the timing of the school year. You see, somewhere between January and April is when most of these crops in the fields and wild fruits are ready for consumption. Since boarding students did not come home at all during this time, they would miss out on the best part of the year. By the time we returned home in April, most of the corn would be dry and the sugar cane would be gone from the fields. One might find some of these things if they were planted late in the season.

At school these fresh foods were not available. At school the corn was only eaten in the form of cornmeal. There are many ways of preparing fresh corn. It can be boiled, roasted on the cob, or crushed and made into a type of bread that can be mixed with sour cream or something like cottage cheese. It can also be shelled from the cob and cooked together with peanuts or beans to make *inkobe*. Shelled corn can be cooked with melons or pumpkins to make *umxhanxa*.

With the first term of the school year coming between January and April, the students missed out on all these wonderful and tasty dishes. There were a few students who packed such things as *ulude*, a popular vegetable that can be cooked and eaten fresh or boiled and dried to preserve. It makes a wonderful dish called *Idobi* when cooked with peanut butter. The very adventurous students packed *amacimbi*. These are caterpillars that feed on certain types of trees. They are seen only at a certain time of the year for a very short period of time. People gather them. They cook them and then let them dry. They make a delicious and excellent high-protein meal.

There was a little problem with carrying all this food. At school we did not have proper cooking facilities. Some of the necessary ingredients were not available. So even if you carried all these goodies, you had to improvise in order to make the right dishes.

An empty metal jar would do for a pot. Salt was sometimes hard to come by, unless you brought it from home. At our house we tried to cover all the bases and anticipate all the possible needs.

We started cracking peanuts at least one week before school started. We also dried the meat in time. The meat was salted before it was left in the sun to dry to make biltong (*umwabha*). The peanuts were salted as they were being roasted. When we got to school, these were rationed carefully to make sure they lasted a good part of the term. By the time all this food was finished, hopefully you would be used to the routine and food at school.

Going to Matopo was exciting for another reason—totally unrelated to school. We went by bus from home to the city of Bulawayo, a treat by itself. We had the opportunity to see the city and do some window shopping since we did not have any money to buy things with. There was tremendous excitement among the mostly countryside students. We had some money to buy cream donuts and a soft drink (*inamnede*). We would not miss this for the world. The city streets were crowded with students in uniforms. Many of them wore their blazers and always traveled in groups chattering like birds nesting at the riverside. They were busy sharing stories of their vacations.

Sometimes the travel plans called for a night in town. This was a big problem for many people. Accommodations were hard to come by. In our case, we spent the night at our cousin's place at Makhokhoba—known also as the old location. He lived in a single room, equivalent to a studio, on Fourth Street near Mkambo, the famous flea market of Bulawayo.

My cousin had lived in this place since 1943. The rent was less than one British pound a month. At that time this was probably equivalent to about $2 USD. This was very high for his income. To save some money he shared this place with another family. It's hard to imagine how two families could share a room barely 10' × 10'. The truth is they did. Their beds were separated by curtains. Somehow, they managed to fit all their belongings in their own section of the room.

Most of the cooking was done outside. But when it rained they used the famous paraffin primer stoves inside the room. It was amazing that there were not more fires considering the flames from the stoves were literally inches away from the curtains. The bathrooms were outside. One bathroom was shared by a number of families on the block.

It was in this one room that somehow two or three of us managed to find room to spend a night en route to school. We slept literally under my cousin's bed. One night in cramped quarters was a small price to pay for the excitement of being in the big city.

There was always a chance of meeting a distant cousin, uncle, or friend who would buy us meat pies, fish and chips, or cream biscuits from Arenel. These were incredible treats. We looked forward to them all year long. If we could have extended our stay in town by one day, we would have gladly done so despite the horrible accommodations. It never happened. The buses ran all night if they had to.

Matopo was quite different from Wanezi in many respects. It was a co-ed school, which was a big change for some of us. It was a welcome, exciting change from the somewhat military conditions of Wanezi.

Newcomers did not have much to fear. There was some teasing, but nothing compared to Wanezi. I suspect that the presence of women tempered the wildness of the boys. On the other hand, the students were older and more mature. They had a lot more on their minds and more interesting things to do than running run around beating up new students.

Many of the rules were similar. There were boundaries beyond which you did not dare stray. There was an additional boundary to observe—the girls' dormitories were strictly forbidden territory. I suppose the opposite was true, that girls were not allowed in the boys' dormitories. We shared classrooms and socialized during recess. Beyond that we essentially lived in two different schools.

When I first went to Matopo in 1960 there was no TV. An attempt was made in 1961–62 to put a TV in the library. This was very exciting for us because we were seeing this thing called a television for the first time. However, the reception was horrible because we were far from town. We were allowed to watch only special programs which were educational in nature. I remember watching Shakespeare's *Macbeth*. That was quite interesting, because Shakespeare was probably the class's favorite author. However, we barely saw black and white shadows. But everybody sat in the library with eyes glued to this magical box. Perhaps this is what encouraged my classmate Ferdinand to become a television reporter later in life. We were just fascinated by the technology.

As at Wanezi, life revolved around religion and education. However, there was no work. There were no fields to cultivate. There were no cows to tend. Now there was time to expand our horizons. There was the recreation hour between supper and evening study time. Some of us gobbled our meals quickly so that we could take our turn at table tennis or chess or shuffleboard. This was the high point of the day for many students. However, the time allotted to these activities was very short.

Some of us also took to music. No instruments were allowed or available except for the church organ. I joined the great twenty-one-voice boys' choir conducted by Mr. Ranold Mpofu. Choir was wonderful, and Mr. Mpofu was an interesting teacher, leader, and conductor. We enjoyed the practice sessions and looked forward to being on stage in church.

Unfortunately, this opportunity to participate in the choir was available to us only in Forms I and II. When we reached Form III, we formed a choir of eight boys. This choir was beset by a number of problems, one of which was the death of one of the students, Ginder Sibanda, a dear friend of mine. Things were just not the same after that.

There were outdoor sports, including soccer, softball, track, high and long jump, javelin, and shot put. The student population was divided into groups so that they could compete against each other. I must admit that this was not my area of greatest interest.

Softball and track were my favorites. I ran the 100-yard dash, the 220, 440, and relay. I think I did pretty well in all of them. What I remember most about these events is our team leader, Mnumzana J. D. Ndlovu. He did his best to make it interesting. I also remember Zephaniah Dube, who I believe was the greatest mile runner of all time. It is a shame that our opportunities were so limited. There is no doubt in my mind that Zephaniah would have easily won the New York marathon if he had only had the opportunity to run.

I remember Mr. J. D. Ndlovu for another reason. He opened a small window to the outside world for us by letting us read his newspaper, which he got from town. I am sure he had no idea how much this meant to us. Given that there was no radio or television for us to listen to, these newspapers kept us connected to the events outside the school. After all, these were turbulent times for the country from a political standpoint. The wave of the struggle for independence was sweeping across Africa. The black people were intensifying their struggle for liberation. But the whites were digging in their heels. They used every tactic and every means available to them to stop the movement.

Political arrests were a daily occurrence. Leaders were detained in prisons or remote centers such as Wawa and Gonakugzinkwa. Many were placed under house arrest or had their movements restricted in a variety of ways. If technology and finances had been available, the colonial regime would have had every man and woman that was suspect wearing an electronic bracelet. Instead, many people were required to report to a police station once or twice a day. The government thought that this way they would limit the movement of the so-called agitators. When this failed, the agitators were hauled away to remote detention centers.

During the school term we could read about these activities only in Mr. Ndlovu's daily newspaper.

There were demonstrations and rallies all over the country. Political parties were banned. Foreigners who participated in the liberation struggle were deported from the country. Things were especially rough in the cities. One wave of demonstrations, which became known as *Zhi*, saw huge numbers of people fleeing the city of Bulawayo. Shops and businesses burned. People walked as much as thirty or forty miles to find safe havens in their country villages.

Even though I did not know it at the time, all these activities ultimately influenced the course of my own life. In the fifties, three countries in Southern Africa—Southern Rhodesia (now Zimbabwe), Northern Rhodesia (now Zambia) and Nyasaland (now Malawi)—had formed a union known as the Federation of Rhodesia and Nyasaland. The struggle for independence by the African peoples in each of these three territories threatened the stability of the union. This, along with many other forces, led to the collapse of the federation in 1961. Each country was left to face the liberation movement within its borders on its own.

Southern Rhodesia had always been the most developed and strongest of the three. When the other two could not contain the liberation forces, they gave in to the independence movement. Zambia and Malawi became independent countries in 1964 and 1965, respectively. The whites sought refuge in Southern Rhodesia.

It was not just a coincidence that the white people sought to fight the forces of liberation from Southern Rhodesia soil. Southern Rhodesia shares a southern border with South Africa, where apartheid had dug in its heels. This is where the concept of the southern fortress came in. They were going to draw a line here in Southern Rhodesia, where the wave of the independence movement was to be stopped at any cost.

They tried very hard. Southern Rhodesia did not achieve its independence for almost another two decades after its federation partners won theirs. Three decades went by before South Africa became independent. How did this affect the course of my life?

When our political parties could not prosecute the struggle from within our borders, they were forced into exile. Once the struggle spilled beyond our borders, there was no stopping how far it went. The globe became our arena of operations. This is how Zimbabweans dispersed to all corners of the world, and my seed found fertile ground in the United States in Minnesota.

Matopo Secondary School was not in an area as remote as Wanezi. In fact, it was not isolated at all. There was a main road that ran between the boys' dormitories and the classrooms. Several buses traveled up and down this road. Many merchants, farmers, and ordinary people drove up and down this road. Mr. Maphosa, a business man in a nearby village, always stopped at the school with his truckload of goods for the store. Those of us who had money were able to buy bread, buns, cookies, and candies from him. This was very helpful because his store was out of bounds.

The school was located about thirty miles from the city of Bulawayo on the main road to Gwanda. It was nestled between the Lukadzi and Silobini Hills on the banks of the Matopo River. On the road from Bulawayo we passed the grave of Mzilikazi, the Zulu general who had led the Ndebele people from Natal to present-day Zimbabwe. He was running away from the Zulu King Tshaka because he had done something for which he would have been killed.

After about twenty years of wandering through the mountains, valleys, and plains of South Africa, Mzilikazi finally settled down near Ntabazinduna in Zimbabwe. He was a great warrior who earned the respect and friendship of early white settlers. Some of his direct descendants attended church at Matopo.

The perimeter of the school was surrounded by villages. There were no old mines, farms, or little towns. All the villages were out of bounds. The students might have been tempted to go and drink home-brewed beer, but the consequences were too severe to even contemplate the idea. Therefore, on Saturday afternoons all students hung around the school doing a variety of things to keep busy.

It was the time when friends sat down at the *idale* and drank tea made from sugar and burnt paper. The *idale* concept was not as developed here as it had been at Wanezi. I do not know why.

This was the time to do laundry. Students washed their clothes by hand. Most of the time, they used cold water in buckets. The irons used to press clothes were not like modem electric pressing irons. They were not even like the irons that most villagers used, which are like an oven filled with coals. These were just a piece of heavy metal that one heated over coals. When it reached a suitable temperature, you cleaned the bottom and used it to press clothes as quickly as possible. When the iron cooled down, you put it back on the fire again, and repeated the process until all the ironing was done. We generally did a splendid job of pressing those khaki shorts and shirts.

Coming to Matopo Secondary School was not like going from one grade to another. There was a sense of climbing up a ladder or even a mountain. The goal was to reach the top. In a sense, the students at Matopo were a select group of individuals with a certain sense of determination and direction. We had come from a wide range of backgrounds and schools. We had generally been the cream of our respective schools. Now it was time to see the crème de la crème. From the word go, we all dug in our heels, determined to hold our position at the top of the class.

We all hoped to reach the Form IV level, the highest level at Matopo. However, we were aware that the double sections of Forms I and II of sixty or seventy students would be reduced to less than twenty-five in the graduating class of Form IV. We all wanted to be among the lucky two dozen. It would take not just brains, but a lot of determination, hard work, and mental focus.

There wasn't much choice of subjects in Form I. Everybody took the same subjects with the exception of mathematics, which meant algebra and geometry. Everybody took arithmetic. While many people shied away from mathematics, it was the juice upon which some of us thrived. We saw this as the subject that would take us to the top of the heap. Those equations and those angles and degrees introduced us to a new language and a new world. It put us up there with the famous mathematicians such as Pythagoras and Newton. We could set ourselves apart from the rest of the students because we were learning something that others knew absolutely nothing about. It was not just a higher level of English literature or religion. It was an entirely new subject. You had to go to school for this one.

Another subject that opened a totally new and fascinating world for me and a few others was science. General science, taught by Reverend Shenk, was absolutely fascinating. I finally learned how to make soap.

I learned what air consists of. I learned plant and animal physiology. I performed experiments in the lab.

First of all, I learned the big word *laboratory* itself. Remember that none of the primary schools at the time had even the semblance of a lab. This was totally new to me. The combination of general science and mathematics was the ultimate challenge for me.

I enjoyed my other subjects: English, religion, Latin, geography, history and Zulu. Latin was exciting because, in our opinion, only educated people understood Latin. We were told that it was essential to know Latin in order to succeed in medicine and law. Of course, this was just up my alley. I had to know Latin in order to be a doctor.

Miss Hansen was a no-nonsense teacher. You had to know your declensions or else you were dead meat. I studied hard and did well in Latin, but four years was enough for me. Throughout it I always had nagging thoughts about learning a dead language.

I loved Zulu, perhaps because it was my language and I was proud of it. It evoked in me a sense of history, a journey into my own ancestry. My forebears came from South Africa with Mzilikazi, king of the Ndebele people. I enjoyed the literature. Mr. Thomas Dube (now Dr. Thomas Msebe Dube) did a super job of teaching the language. He told us then that he was preparing us to pass not just Form I, but Form IV. We took it all in like dry sponges in a puddle of water. We were thirsty for knowledge.

The only subject that I did not much care for was history. It turned me off. I could not relate very well to the Stone Age and many aspects of history that we were being taught. It seemed to me that it had no relevance to my life or future. As a result, when I got to Form III, where I had the opportunity to drop one subject, there was no question in my mind which had to go: history.

Interestingly enough, I began to read history on my own. I read history books that seemed to have relevance to my life, such as the history of the Zulus, the Ndebeles, slavery, the trade routes, and the early explorers. In these topics I learned something about my past and my ancestors. I learned something about the events that have shaped the world in which we live. I read about the scramble for Africa that created the disastrous boundaries of present day Africa. I read about slavery and understood the civil rights movement. I put Dr. Martin Luther King in proper context. History became real to me. I have found it fascinating ever since.

When I dropped history, I was able to take additional science, which enhanced my understanding of general science. Only four of us were brave enough to venture in that direction. Unfortunately only two of us, Simon Malinga and I, completed the course at Form IV level. One of the original four was my best friend and lab partner, Ginder Sibanda, who died when we were in Form III. He was a very bright, lively young man and a fun, loving human being. We had been not just lab partners; Ginder and I had a passion for table tennis (ping pong) and chess. We ate our food very fast in order to get to the recreation room early and secure our spot at one of the games. He had a slight advantage in table tennis because he was tall and lanky. His arms were much longer than mine. Even though he won most of the time, I did get my share of good games. The joy of it all was just plain fun and relaxation from our primary task: studying.

He was a super guy, a wonderful friend to be with. That recreation hour was probably the best time of the entire day. It was time well spent. When the bell rang for us to go to our classrooms to study in the evening, we were ready. Our minds were cleared of the day's clutter. We were ready to read and concentrate on whatever we were doing. In general, those of us that played the most during the recreation period did better in school. That may be an exaggeration, but I know it was very good for me.

Matopo was a great academic institution. Even though religion was its primary mission, education was given its share of importance. There were classes practically all day except for a few periods here and there. These periods when there were no classes were taken up by library time, sports, or one of the skill courses such as carpentry, gardening, or some other hands-on skill.

The teachers were excellent as proven by the performance of their students at national and international level examinations. We had a major examination at Form II level. Many students went to train for various careers after this examination. Doing well in this examination was critical. It probably determined their destiny as far as what they could do academically and ultimately careerwise. One had to do well to secure a place in one of the twenty-four slots in Form III. Considering that Matopo took in students from other schools as well for the Form III class, there were probably more like eighteen or twenty slots for the Matopo graduates. Competition was fierce. Two sections in Form I and two sections in Form II would be whittled down to a mere twenty-four students.

How did we accomplish this seemingly impossible task? There was a tremendous amount of structure to a student's life at school. There were morning prayers; there was breakfast; then there was a whole day full of classes and other activities. There was supper followed by the famous recreation hour. After that there was the evening study time, which was supervised, to make sure that there was peace and quiet. At the end of the evening, which at about 8:30 p.m. was fairly early, we went to the dormitories and got ready for bed. When the bell rang at 9:00 p.m. there was stone silence—unless, of course, one was asking for trouble. The prefects were always there to give demerits to anyone who did not follow the rules.

In this program there was little room for idle time. Of course, many students did not like it. They thought it was too restrictive. On the other hand, what could we have done with the free time? We were not allowed beyond the boundaries. This was not a supercharged, sports-oriented school. Life revolved around religion and education.

On Saturday mornings we were assigned various duties around the school. I remember my assignment was to clear the weeds and cultivate the flower gardens around the female staff quarters. This was actually an interesting opportunity. For one thing, we had a chance to be out of bounds legally. We had a chance to see the girls outside the classrooms, although we could not really talk to them. We also had the opportunity to talk and get to know some of our teachers outside of the classroom. This may have seemed to be a minor thing at the time, but it helped some of us to build enduring friendships with our former teachers. Many of them are still at Messiah College in Harrisburg, Pennsylvania.

Saturday work lasted only until noon. The rest of the day we were free to do as we pleased, but always within the boundaries. This was the time to wash and iron our clothes. More importantly, it was time to write letters to our families and friends back home. My father was very good at writing and replying to our letters. My mother, too, always took time to write or ask someone else to write for her. Their letters were very special. I felt a sense of connectedness whenever I received them, like I was at home again, even though I knew I could not have that delicious home-cooked meal. So whenever I got a chance I wrote them letters and told them about my studies and all sorts of student activities that I had been involved in. Many of us came from the same general area. Some of their parents were my parents' friends or even relatives. So, in my letters I always told my parents about these friends and how we got along. I believe that this gave them a sense of comfort, assuring them that I was not alone, unhappy, or lonely. They also knew that if there ever was any problem, my friends would take care of me and they would be sure to tell my parents. It was that communal atmosphere in which I was raised. I also wrote letters to my brothers and sisters. The more letters you wrote the more you were likely to receive.

When the mail came, the senior prefect would call out the names on each piece of mail in the dining room. This was a special time because each piece of mail was like a small window to the outside world. It was a chance to learn about all the family affairs and the social and political developments most relevant to me. It might even be a chance to hear from a girlfriend left at home. So this was big time.

On the other hand, this may have been a very depressing time for those students who never got any mail. They may not have received any mail because they did not write to anybody. They may not have received any mail because their parents did not know how to read or write. Some students came from such remote areas that no mail ever got there or ever came from there. For these students, unless they heard indirectly about their parents, there would be no contact for about three months at a time. The school terms ran from January to April for the first term, from May to August for second term, and from September to December for the third term. There was a two- or three-week holiday between the first and second and between the second and third terms, and about a month in December.

This end-of-the-year holiday was especially exciting because Christmas was coming. It also was the end of whatever grade you were in. Most of us would have passed that grade. We may even have done very well. So we had great news for our family. There were generally no assignments over this holiday, since we would be starting a new grade with new teachers in January. It was a real vacation to just have fun.

Most industries closed for the Christmas and New Year celebrations, and many people had a chance to go home and get together with family and friends.

No one made telephone calls during the school year. Even if the school had a telephone, it would have been useless because telephones did not exist in the villages, nor even in many small towns. There would be no place to call. I was twenty-two years old when I used a telephone for the first time in my life, when I worked for the city council in Bulawayo as a clerk. It was an incredible experience. The thought of my voice carried by wire clear across town was a miracle. Today I sit in America and call the most remote part of Zimbabwe and instantly get a clear voice answering the phone. It is hard to explain to my children how far technology has come just in my lifetime.

Since there were no televisions, no telephones, and no Gameboys, we sat around and talked. No wonder we got to know each other so well. We were also able to build long-lasting friendships. Of course, some people spent their Saturdays reading. But for the most part, Saturday afternoon was a day to relax.

Sunday was a different story. Since life in the school revolved around education and religion, Sunday was the big day for church activities. There were morning prayers, Sunday school, the church service, and evening prayers. We participated in all these activities in various capacities. Sometimes we read the scriptures, prayed, or sang. At one time I was an usher at the main service. This was a nice job. You got to meet and know a lot of people from the school and the community. We led people to their seats in the church. I rather enjoyed the church services, especially the music.

On the Sunday before the end of the school year we sang Christmas songs. I enjoyed this very much. The last year that I was at Matopo I was one of the students who sang. My part was to sing a solo as one of the three kings walking up the aisle. It was quite an experience.

But Sunday also posed a dilemma for me sometimes. You see, I was raised in the Seventh Day Adventist Church as a child. It was the church to which my mother and my brothers and sisters belonged. We observed all the rules and regulations of the SDA Church at home. That meant we worshiped on Saturday. We did not work on Saturday. We did not eat pork and so on. The dilemma goes back to my Standard IV year, when I broke ranks and went to boarding school in a Brethren in Christ Church School instead of the SDA School. I did not get to be baptized in the SDA Church as it would have happened if I had gone to Solusi Mission. Well, I did not get baptized in the Brethren in Christ Church either, since I felt that it was not really my family church. There were occasions on Sundays when only baptized members could attend. In my last year at Matopo all but three of us were baptized members of the church. We would walk out and find something else to do somewhere.

This did not matter at the next school I attended. It was a government school and therefore non-denominational, the equivalent of public school in America.

Four years went by rather quickly at Matopo. I made it through Forms I, II, and III to reach the highest grade in the school, Form IV. Only about half the students in that class had started with me in Form I. The rest joined us at Form III from other schools. We took our final examination in November 1963, just about the time that President John F. Kennedy died. The sadness was matched only by the intensity with which we prepared for this examination. It was then known as the A-Level examination, produced and graded by Cambridge University in England. This examination was the equivalent of a high school diploma. But for us it was much more than that. It determined whether you went on to college. It determined whether you got into a technical school. Basically, your whole future was determined by how well you did in this examination.

Some of us put a few pennies together and bought paraffin. With that we could make lamps out of a tin can and an old piece of cloth, preferably cotton from a T-shirt. We would get up very early in the morning, around three or four, and study by the light of these lamps. We were all well aware of the fact that the African (non-white) students from all over the country had only two schools for the A-Level (Forms V and VI). Only one of these schools, Goromonzi, was co-ed. Fletcher High was for boys only. The pyramid was getting narrower.

One had to pass A-Level examinations to go to the only university in the country, the University College of Rhodesia.

At the end of 1963, we said good-bye to each other and our teachers, not knowing what the future would bring each of us. We all hoped for the best but prepared for the worst. I applied for a teaching position within the Brethren in Christ Church school system just in case I did not do well enough to go on to Form V. I did get a post at Nyumbane primary school. I taught Standard 4, the equivalent of fifth or sixth grade. It was an exciting job, my first real job. I even bought my first necktie and wristwatch with the money that I earned. I was paid £25.00, or about $50.00 a month. This was a lot of money in those days. The temptation to continue teaching was great. But I knew that this would not get me to the top of the mountain that I had created for myself.

The headmaster of the school was a gentleman by the name of Mr. Matshiya. He had been a teacher for many years. Even though he did not have much education, his years of experience more than made up for it. He was an administrator who ruled with an iron fist. His word was the law of the school for both students and teachers. This was probably a good thing, because there was never a problem with discipline in the school. Any student who entertained ideas of misbehaving stopped short once they thought of the wrath of Mr. Matshiya. Students did not dare come late to school because they knew how much trouble they would be in. The parents also knew that they had to make sure that their children were in school on time and ready to learn. Deep down this man really cared about his students, teachers, and parents. He took his job seriously. I came to know and understand him better many years later, after he retired from teaching.

One day in February 1964 my father drove up to the school late in the afternoon. At first I thought perhaps something had happened. But when I looked at him he appeared happy. So I knew that it was not sad news. He had received my A-Level results.

I had done very well—well enough to go on to Form V. This meant I had to leave my job and go back to school. I was a bit sad to leave my post. I had become attached to my students and I enjoyed teaching. However, with my eyes and mind focused on the peak of that mountain, it was time to go up one step on the ladder.

# Chapter 5

# Fletcher High School 1964–1965

❋   ❋   ❋   ❋   ❋   ❋

Fletcher High School was a government boys' school located in the Midlands. It was a few miles east of Gwelo, then the third largest city in Zimbabwe. For me this was a bit like going back to Wanezi Mission, where I had done Standard 5 and 6, also a boys' school. But Fletcher was different in many respects.

The students were much older. These were students in Forms III, IV, V and VI. There was a mixture of students from all over the country. There was even a mixture of languages: Ndebele, Shona, Soto, and others. There was not as much of the "big brother" relationship between newcomers and returning students. Each one of us was very much on his own. Granted, there were small cliques here and there. For the most part, this was a place where you developed your friends based largely upon classroom associations or dormitory arrangements.

The upperclassmen, Forms V and VI students, had their own blocks of dormitories on the eastern side of the school. Forms III and IV students lived in the dorms on the western side. However, we all ate in the common dining hall. Because of these living arrangements and our different classes, we did not get to mix with one another much.

We had times when we participated in sports together. In fact, we were divided into groups, known as houses, which competed against each other in sports. I did well in swimming for my house. However, this was not a major part of a student's life. There were many good soccer players in the school. Many of these had played soccer in their previous school.

We had other forms of entertainment such as ballroom dancing, even though there were no women with whom to dance. We toyed with the idea of asking girls from a nearby training college to our school. However, there were a few problems with that, mainly that there were only a handful of girls there. But there were no strict boundaries like we had at Wanezi and Matopo.

There was an understanding that students should live and be within the school grounds during certain hours of the day. However, students were able to go into town, Gwelo, when they wanted. Most of us did not go anywhere because we did not know anybody in this part of the country. Even if we had known people, we probably would not have had enough money or time to go anywhere. This freedom of movement meant that we were not shut out from the outside world.

There was a lot going on in the country at this time. Politically, the country was experiencing probably its biggest challenge ever. The federation had dissolved. Southern Rhodesia was on its own. The wave of the independence movement coming from the north was threatening to engulf this country, too. The British colonial power appeared to be ready to let go and allow the country to be independent under African rule. However, the white colonialists were not ready. They were prepared to fight to the bitter end. They had already taken drastic measures, such as to ban the African political parties ZAPU and ZANU. This had forced the liberation movement to set up operating centers outside the country in the newly independent countries such as Tanzania and Ghana. To strengthen their resolve even further, the whites had turned to a staunch defender of what they considered to be their rights. His name was Ian Douglas Smith.

He owned a farm not too far from Fletcher High School. This man was prepared to stave off African rule by any means necessary. He repeated "No majority rule today or ever" in every speech.

The black African population was overwhelmingly in the majority in the country. Mr. Smith managed to hold the tide of independence from overrunning Zimbabwe for about sixteen years. In the meantime, the viciousness of the struggle for independence created deep divisions among the African leaders. There was no agreement on the best tactics to use against the colonial regime. These divisions permeated the country. Of course, our student population was not immune to them either. There was so much bitterness that a major tragedy occurred at school.

One student died in one of these altercations. Similar occurrences were reported in cities across the country. Those political leaders that had not been arrested, detained, or forced out of the country formed what was called the People's Caretaker Council. This was an organization put together partly to continue the struggle for liberation, but more importantly, to keep the people together and heal the wounds that were dividing us. This was a tall order for any organization. It was even more difficult for this organization to function because the white government was more determined than ever to resist majority rule.

In 1965 we stood on the balcony of our dormitory and listened as Prime Minister Ian Smith announced a Unilateral Declaration of Independence of Southern Rhodesia from Great Britain. In a speech that seemed to have been lifted from the American Declaration of Independence, Ian Smith was emphatic about the white population's determination to fight against any attempt to grant the majority in the country the right to self-determination. He was unwavering in his own resolve to do whatever would be required to stop the black people from taking over the government. With that announcement, the lives of millions of people in Zimbabwe and its neighbors were changed forever.

Great Britain immediately asked the United Nations to impose economic sanctions against its estranged colony. What had hitherto been a non-violent struggle for self-determination by the African majority suddenly took on a military stance. The exiled political parties and leadership of the African blacks set up guerrilla training camps abroad. Young men and women fled the country in droves to fill these camps. They were angry, frustrated, and determined to return with weapons with which to drive their oppressors out to sea, if need be. Ian Smith and his people were equally determined, with the assistance of the South African whites, to build a southern fortress. They vowed to fight to the last man.

Britain, on the other hand, was trying all kinds of alternatives to bring its outlaw colony back into the fold and thus salvage some of its power and pride. The United Nations intensified its economic sanctions. The masses were caught in the middle, having nothing to defend themselves with and nowhere to go.

For fifteen long years, the war and its sanctions took its toll. Families were torn apart by death and destruction across the country. Parents and children were separated by arrests, torture, and the disappearance of loved ones. Hordes of schoolchildren streamed across the borders and poured into refugee camps. Unlike Bosnia, much of this happened away from the eye of the camera. Untold millions of horror stories and untold human suffering went unreported. Those stories will be read only in the history books of the birds, the trees, and the animals that watched in horror. Only the ants know how many shallow graves lie in the mountains, valleys, and plains across the country.

In 1965 we huddled in groups, small and large, pondering what the Unilateral Declaration of Independence meant for us and, more importantly, what it meant for our future.

The answers were hard to come by. We were thirsty for education. We had worked hard to come from all the small and large schools across the country to reach this level, available at only two schools in the whole country. Were we going to lose it all right here and now? That path toward medical school, which had opened up ever so slightly, suddenly seemed to be shutting down at an accelerated pace.

The sun came up again the next morning. We went back to the classrooms. As I recall, there were some minor demonstrations at the school and in the nearby township. But for the most part life at the school went on without much disruption. The school principal was a tall, hard-nosed, elderly white man, Mr. Knottenbelt. He had a heavy, raspy voice that struck terror in many students' hearts. He towered above just about every teacher and every student as he strolled up and down the corridors of the school. There is no doubt that he feared for the safety of the students during those tense moments of Mr. Smith's Unilateral Declaration of Independence. He must have been praying for peace even as he displayed an air of confidence in his ability to keep things under control. He was indeed an old man, but kept a steady hand at the controls.

I did not have the pleasure of having him for a teacher. However, I was told that he was a brilliant mathematician. He taught students in the lower forms. They seemed to enjoy mathematics whenever he was the teacher. I found out that Mr. Knottenbelt eventually joined the faculty at the University of Rhodesia and he was put in charge of one of the student residences.

I have rather dull memories of the academic aspects of my life at Fletcher High. One thing that sticks out as being interesting was our math classes in Form V. We had the famous Mr. Chad for our teacher, a rather colorful gentleman in his own way. He always carried this big leather briefcase around the school. When he came to our class he laid the briefcase on the table and took out a textbook. You see, there was this excellent math textbook which had instructive examples of problems worked out in detail. Mr. Chad opened the textbook to the page where the lesson for the day was to be found. He put the opened book behind his briefcase and proceeded to lecture as he glanced at the book from time to time. The problem was that if he was asked a question that did not have an example outlined in the textbook, he was lost. As a human being, he was an amiable fellow who did not say much.

One day we decided to ask him what he did before he came to Fletcher High. It turned out that he had been a soldier in the British Army in India. When he retired from the army, he was given a teaching position in one of the British colonies. We were the guinea pigs upon whom Mr. Chad was going to hone his math teaching skills. Even though Mr. Chad was not the greatest teacher in the world, we had a lot of fun in his class. There was not much to remember about most of the classes.

One interesting event that I recall was a visit by an African-American man. I am not sure what his academic background was. However, he came to demonstrate and lecture about the space program. He had an impressive model of Sputnik. He demonstrated how scientists were planning to carry out projects to send spaceships to the moon. The idea was to show us that the theories that we were learning could be and actually were being put to use. He made the whole theory of gravitational forces and the solar system much more real and understandable. Those of us who were already interested in the sciences were in our glory. What once seemed so abstract now appeared very real. It was possible to send someone to the moon and they would not fall back to earth. Questions were popping up everywhere in our heads.

I do not know if this had been done deliberately or not, but to see someone of our color traveling around the world demonstrating such high-powered science was a huge morale booster. Many of us had dreams of being scientists. However, everywhere we looked, the top scientists were white. Granted, we had some black science teachers, but they were few and far between. This often left us wondering whether our first objective should be to struggle for equality or to strive for a better education with the hope that we would get recognition by virtue of our achievements.

This question was very real in the minds of many young people during the sixties in Zimbabwe. It came as no surprise then that many young people left the country before completing high school or shortly thereafter. The presence of one of us at the school gave us hope that there was room out there in the world of science for us. We were the future rocket scientists. There are many science teachers scattered around the country today that are products of Fletcher High. There are also a number of medical doctors who came through the same school. All we did was study.

It was at Fletcher High where I picked up the bad habit of smoking cigarettes. At that time I believe there was a combination of factors that influenced me and others. Zimbabwe has always been a big producer of tobacco, and along with that there has been a tremendous amount of cigarette advertising. Of course, most of it was directed at getting young people who would be long-term consumers to start smoking. Smoking cigarettes was glamorized. It was a status symbol. Smoking cigarettes meant that one had money or had achieved a social level above the crowd. It was a thing that people did in order to keep their brains sharp while studying. We knew nothing about the manipulation of people's minds and habits through advertising. However, someone in the tobacco industry certainly knew something about marketing. The cigarette company sales representatives were all over the country in beautiful cars. They were some of the highest paid among people with high school educations. I was caught in their net.

State Express was the brand that I smoked. It was magnificently packaged. But if the intent was to keep me hooked, they failed miserably. Fortunately, three years later I found my senses and quit smoking. I have never smoked a cigarette since and I don't miss it. I do not know if smoking had anything to do with it, but I recall a few miserable days that I spent in the infirmary. I had an upper respiratory ailment that knocked me off my feet. I went to the nurse and she decided to keep me in the infirmary for a few days. I have no idea what medication she was giving me. Now that I know a thing or two about medicine, it would be interesting to see what she wrote in my file.

My two years at Fletcher High school soon came to an end. I had worked very hard. My mind was still focused on the top of that mountain where I was going to pick up the letters *M* and *D* to attach to my name. We took the examinations in November, I believe. Once again we all departed and headed back to our various homes, hoping for the best but prepared for the worst. The next stop if everything went well would be the citadel of higher learning, the University College of Rhodesia.

I went home much the same way as I had done at the end of Form IV, filled with hope. I had studied hard and thought I had done well. On the other hand, many brilliant students had stumbled at the A-Level. When I got home I told my parents that even if I did well enough to go to the university, which I thought was likely, I had about three months to kill. I thought it would be a good idea to look for a temporary job and make some money. I went back to my hometown of Bulawayo, where the regional education offices were located. There I talked to a few education officers about the possibility of getting a teaching post. There seemed to be nothing available for such a short time.

One day I came upon an office building which housed the church and school offices for AME church. I went in and explained my situation to them. It just so happened that they were looking for somebody for one of their schools located across the Gwaai River, on the way to the Victoria Falls. This was a remote, hot, sandy area. I guess they were having trouble finding people to go there. I immediately accepted the offer.

The very next day, I was on the train on my way to Mpindo Primary School. I had never been in this part of the country before. Mpindo is located about a hundred miles north of Bulawayo. The ride on a coal train was practically an all-day trip. The train stopped in every town, or so it seemed. I looked outside to catch the scenery. However, after a while this became boring. I could not fall asleep because I was afraid that I would miss my stop. Finally, late in the afternoon, we pulled up to a stop in what seemed to me to be the middle of nowhere. I do not remember if there was even a single building. This, I was told, was Mpindo station. I was glad I had reached my final destination.

On the other hand, I did not like the idea of being dropped off in this jungle. My fellow passengers were kind enough to direct me to the school. It was not far from the train station. However, because of the sand, getting there was a trip and a half.

A tall, slender gentleman by the name of Paul Sibanda was expecting somebody. He was the headmaster of the school. I handed him a letter of introduction from headquarters. He quickly arranged for young fellows to help me with my luggage as he took me to my house. This was a small, square, brick structure. The floor was made of cement. The roof was grass thatched. There was not a single piece of furniture in there. I was somewhat prepared for this venture. I had brought my blankets and a straw mat to make my bed on the floor. I brought a pot, some corn meal, meat, salt, sugar, and teabags. Those were basic necessities with which I would survive until I got my bearings. Things actually turned out to be not too bad.

Mr. Sibanda was very friendly. He showed me the ropes. He took me to the classrooms that were almost as empty as my sleeping quarters. They had wooden benches, desks, and almost nothing else. I was given Standard 5 to teach. Again, with the help of Mr. Sibanda, this was easy. It was the day-to-day living that was hard to get used to.

Paul took me around to the villages after school and introduced me to the homeowners and the area. We walked to the grocery store and met the owner. He was our lifeline because we could order things from town and send letters to the post office in town through him.

One afternoon Paul took me to meet a certain gentleman who was a well-respected medicine man with the same last name as Paul. When we got there, Mr. Sibanda was busy on his knees in his yard, with a ruler in hand and a number of women and children around him. He seemed to be measuring some cloth material and cutting pieces from a big roll. You see, Mr. Sibanda was in a polygamous marriage; he had ten wives. I am not certain how many children he had, but there were quite a few. As the good provider that he was, he was giving out pieces of material for the women and children to make clothes for themselves. It was quite a sight to say the least.

Mr. Sibanda interrupted his activity to meet with us. He was a short, slender gentleman with an engaging, effusive personality. He showed us his medical office, which had an incredible assortment of herbs, roots, jars, bones, and a whole lot more. However, to his credit, everything was arranged neatly in some order which I am sure only he knew. He had just started construction of what was to be his new medical office next to the old one. The new one was made of bricks. Obviously, it was going to be a very modern medical office. I was told that he had a thriving practice. He definitely needed it to support his very large family.

He also proudly showed us his fields. He had several acres of land with a corn crop that extended as far as your eyes could see. A huge tractor was parked at the entrance. This man knew what he had to do, and he did it well. His family had plenty of food to eat as long as the rains came. I had the pleasure of having some of his children as my students.

Polygamy was prevalent in those days. At that time I did not see it as anything out of the ordinary because it was part of the culture in which I grew up. However, as I have grown older and lived away from it, I have become curious to understand it. One thing that I have observed in retrospect and on many visits to Zimbabwe is the loyalty factor in these polygamous families. It was rare to find situations where the women left their husbands. In some situations even after the husband died the women remained together.

Another observation is the tightness of the family as far as the children from the different mothers are concerned. They shared everything as brothers and sisters, oftentimes even better than children from monogamous families. Someday I would like to study and understand in detail how this social phenomenon evolved and what made it work.

Being a teacher was a fulfilling job. Teachers were probably the most respected people in the community. Apart from knowing that what you were doing would benefit your students and the nation for years to come, you were rewarded by getting incredible respect from the community. As Paul and I traveled around the community on our after-school trips we met people from all walks of life in the villages. The people we met ranged from the village chief to the local alcoholics who wandered from village to village in search of beer.

There is a kind of beer that is traditionally brewed using cornmeal and other grains used as yeast. It was popular in the area around the school. The recipe for making the beer is simple. The ingredients are available to practically everybody. The process takes four to seven days. There may be slight variations depending upon circumstances and ingredients available at the time. The ingredients are basically corn and another grain called *rapoko*, which serves as the yeast. The proportions may differ.

This beer has been commercialized. It is produced by the breweries in all cities and municipalities and is sold in the beer gardens. The problem is that the beer does not always taste the same. Some people know how to make it better than others. As a result, when Mrs. X brews her beer, everybody wants to go to her house because she produces the best.

People generally get very drunk on this stuff. Thankfully, the weather is generally warm, especially in the area where Mpindo is located, so people can simply fall asleep pretty much where they want, whether it is inside the house or outside. Traditionally, people drank this beer from large clay pots or from large gourds. The pot or gourd would be passed around from one person to the next, with everybody sitting in a circle. There are big questions about the health aspects of this practice. However, it was actually the comradeship of sharing that brought people to these gatherings in the first place. The have-nots of the community always found a way to share a beer with someone.

Stopping this tradition for health reasons would probably tear at the basic fabric of the society. Heavy drinking was always condemned or at least discouraged. I got to meet a few people at these beer parties after they'd had a few too many drinks. They talked nonstop. But they were often entertaining.

This was probably a healthy thing in itself because otherwise there were not many other forms of entertainment. There were no movies. In fact, I venture to say 80 percent of the people had never seen a movie. There were no theaters. There were no sports complexes or gyms for the community except for the primary school soccer field. Of course, there was no TV to watch.

After visiting the community I would come back to my one room. I would cook using a primer stove. This was a small stove top that used pressurized paraffin lit by a match. The meals were generally simple. Most of the time, I would make our national staple food: cornmeal porridge or stew with or without a vegetable.

The cornmeal porridge is made by boiling water. Once the water starts boiling, you add cornmeal and stir the pot to mix it. Keep adding cornmeal until the porridge is quite thick. Then cover the pot and let it simmer for a while. In the meantime you could be cooking your stew or vegetables. After a few minutes—I say a few minutes deliberately because no one ever looks at the clock—stir the porridge and add more cornmeal as needed. If the stew is ready, the whole meal is ready. The porridge is then dished onto a platter.

In days gone by, porridge was eaten with bare hands. Several people shared the same plate. Each one would scoop out a mouthful-sized portion of the porridge and mold it with one hand into a nice little ball. Then you take this ball and dip it lightly in the stew and put it in your mouth. Some people still insist on eating porridge by hand because they say it tastes better that way. The truth of the matter is that it probably tastes the same whether one uses a spoon or a fork.

For many people, this is what their lunch and dinner consisted of most of the time. There is more variety in the summertime. There is fresh corn, peanuts, melons, pumpkins, and a number of other crops in the fields. These can be combined in many ways to make various dishes. Some of these things do not require any cooking at all. Others need only to be steamed or boiled briefly. Cooking was never my favorite pastime. Therefore, I chose to eat those foods that required minimum time near the fire. Mealtime was probably the most frustrating time of my day.

We used outdoor pit latrines. I had an encounter with a little *inhlangwane* snake one day. You see, our toilet had a wooden fence around it. One afternoon after using the toilet I stepped out from the fence, and right there in front of me, literally standing on its tail, was a feisty little snake. This little thing almost gave me a heart attack. It stood there hissing and staring straight at me. I am terrified of snakes to begin with. This day was almost enough to make me pack my bags and leave. I froze. This was probably a good reaction because I suppose the snake did not feel threatened. It quickly got down and slithered away.

From that day on I looked carefully before I entered or exited the toilet. Those were the hazards of life in the countryside. I often wonder why there were not many cases of snake poisoning reported. To this day my fear of snakes persists. I am even afraid of snakes that I see on television.

My stay at Mpindo Primary School was brief. Shortly after I got there I received my results from Fletcher High School. I was ecstatic when I found out that I had done well enough at the A-Level to proceed to the university. Even though I had not been accepted into medical school, this was wonderful news. After fourteen years of hard work, this was indeed a great achievement. I was among only a handful of students from around the country who had made it into the university.

I left Mpindo without any hesitation even though I loved my students and the villagers. I almost missed the train because I woke up late. It was due at our train station between three and four in the morning. Getting to the station was not easy because of the sand on the road. Running was almost impossible. However, I managed to get into one of the last cars at the back of the train as it sounded the horn signaling its departure. And so my adventures at Mpindo came to an end as the Wankie coal train pulled away, headed for the city of Bulawayo.

I was still so excited about my results and the prospects of going to the university that the journey seemed much shorter. Before I knew it I was home, sharing the excitement with my parents. There was no doubt in my mind that they were proud of my accomplishments. They had every reason to be.

I was the first one in my family that was going to enter the university. I was also the first one from our area, for miles around, who was going to the University College of Rhodesia. Up until then this had been a place reserved for the privileged few whites. My parents had worked hard to put all of us through school. Every achievement by their children was a gratifying reward for their efforts. I shall forever be indebted to them for their wisdom, their sweat, and their unwavering support and encouragement. *May they rest in peace.*

*Chapter 6*

# The University College of Rhodesia 1966–1967

※　※　※　※　※　※

O
n March 12, 1966, I boarded a train once again at the Bulawayo train station. I had done this many times before when I attended Fletcher High and during my stay at Mpindo. This time it was only fitting and perhaps symbolic of my accomplishments that I was going to go past Fletcher High to the next station. The train was bound for Salisbury, now known as Harare.

It was an overnight journey on the coal train. I had a third-class ticket, which was slightly better than fourth class (known as *umbombela*) in that there were bunk beds. A few of my former classmates were on the train, so the journey was not lonely.

There was not much of any scenery to enjoy since the whole trip was at night. It took twelve hours to cover three hundred miles. That explains why the fireman (the man who shoveled the coal into the engine) was paid very well. Twelve hours is a long time to be hanging around fire. I don't think any of us slept that night.

There was a lot of excitement about the prospects of being a college student. I must also point out that we had reservations about being at the university as well. This was going to be our first experience in a multiracial school. Unfortunately, it could not have come at a worse time. There were tremendous political and racial tensions in the country. The college was known to be a hotbed of political activity.

You see, the University College of Rhodesia was an affiliate of London University. As such, it had been given some autonomy within the college campus. I suppose they had been granted this status because the very idea of having racially mixed dormitories and classrooms violated every written and unwritten law in the country. Races simply did not mix.

At any rate, wanted, accepted or not, invited or not, we were there on our own merits. We were going to find a way to be accepted. Out of about a thousand students, there were about two hundred black Africans.

There were three residence halls: Manfred Hall and Casaunders Hall for men; Swinton Hall for women. I was assigned to Casaunders Hall. They had done an excellent job of scattering different races in the three dormitories. I do not know what formula they used.

Each hall was self-sufficient. It had student rooms, a kitchen, dining room, and lounge. I must say that the treatment we received as far as accommodations and dining facilities were concerned was better than in many five-star hotels. We were given clean linens and towels every day. We did not have to make our beds or clean our rooms. There was a waiter in a clean, white uniform who escorted us to our table in the dining room. Each meal consisted of several courses, even breakfast.

If they brought you something that you did not like, they would gladly get you something of your choice. The meals were unbelievable. They were out of this world. We never saw cornmeal porridge at the university.

We had mid-morning and mid-afternoon tea or coffee and snacks. These were almost a meal in themselves. There was tea or coffee in the lounge after dinner.

This heavenly treatment concealed the tensions on campus. There was a student center where everyone hung out when they were not in classes, which even had a bar, and also a student union office.

Shortly after school started there were preparations for elections of officers for the student union. In this racially charged atmosphere, constitutional issues of equal representation quickly arose. This escalated into a big debate, and there were near riots during the elections. At one point the ballot box was stolen, causing the elections to become null and void.

This was a reflection of the racial tension within the country as a whole. Ever since the Declaration of Independence in 1965 by Ian Smith, the country was, for all intents and purposes, at war. Among the many efforts to prevent majority rule, strict emergency powers had been invoked by the government. There was a crowd control measure that said a gathering of more than three people within three feet of each other constituted a crowd. This effectively meant that there could not be any political rallies that were not sanctioned by the government.

However, as we all knew, there were a million and one reasons why the government would deny such a permit. Without political rallies it was difficult to organize the masses. For a while the university was somewhat exempt from all this. Since it was a multiracial institution, under normal circumstances, what applied to the black students would apply to the white students. From about the third week after school started, there were demonstrations, rallies, and meetings all over campus. Some rallies were held on the soccer field where people could stand three feet apart and thus get around the crowd rule. Pretty soon things escalated to the point where police were called on campus. This in itself became a hot issue, which brought in people who otherwise would have stayed on the sidelines. Asking police to come into the campus was a violation of the university's charter.

For days, weeks, and months there were demonstrations all over campus. I recall one day when we attempted to block the classrooms and prevent people from entering, the police were there in full force. They had police dogs, handcuffs, and clubs. Their commander announced that he was going to give us three chances to disperse. He gave one command. Of course nobody moved. He gave the second command, and again nobody moved. He gave the third command, and when nobody moved he ordered the police to let the dogs loose.

We were standing at the entrance to one of the science classrooms. On the side of the entrance there was a six- to eight-foot drop to the lower level. There was pandemonium as the dogs attacked. The police charged with clubs. Many of us jumped down onto the ledge as if it were only two feet high.

There is a lot to be said for the courage of youth and their determination to gain freedom. This brutality only fueled the anger of the university community. There was not much learning going on under these conditions even though the college tried to maintain a semblance of normalcy. However, there was just too much going on.

I recall another demonstration outside the Parliament building in Harare. Once again we tried to avoid the crowd rule of more than three people within three feet of each other. Things went rather well until we attempted to block the entrance to Parliament. We had actually hoped to enter the building, if possible. The police unleashed a tremendous amount of force and violence, not just to stop the demonstration, but to break it up.

Once they blocked us from entering Parliament, they let the dogs loose and came after us with clubs. As we scattered all over the place, they chased some of us and made several arrests.

I recall a friend of mine who ran in the same direction as I did was arrested. As the dogs were chasing us, we came upon a ledge. He jumped and fell. The dogs caught him and the police picked him up and tossed him into their Land Rover jeep. This was the dreaded police vehicle used in those days. They even had protective wire mesh on the windows. Leonard and others were released after interrogation.

In the midst of all this chaos and confusion, there was life for the students apart from politics. The university campus was quite a distance from downtown Harare. Many of us did not have cars. There were two ways to get into town. The expensive and sure way was to call a taxi, which usually came quickly. The other way, more popular with many of us, was to hitchhike.

There was no telling what type of vehicle would stop for you. I recall one day when a huge truck carrying pigs stopped. We hopped in and made our way into town. There were no buses that you could count on. Many students had a small allowance available to them after buying books and other supplies. So on weekends we went into town, even if it meant just to go window shopping.

Sometimes we went to see soccer matches at Gwanzura Stadium. The Highlanders and Dynamos were popular teams. One was from Bulawayo and the other was based in Harare. They provided the best entertainment.

Sometimes we went to the horse races in Borrowdale. My cousin enjoyed this sport a great deal. I eventually came to enjoy it too. It was interesting that the cousin I lived with in Bulawayo loved horse racing; and then in Harare I found another cousin that was equally interested in horse races. The good thing about this sport was that we would be outdoors in open air.

Apart from watching the horses and the excitement associated with it, we shared drinks and just relaxed. I was never much of a beer drinker even back then, but I enjoyed a cold Castle beer or Lion beer on a hot Saturday afternoon.

Every now and then on a Saturday afternoon, I would go to Arcadia where my cousin lived. When he finished work at noon, he would buy some beer and we would just sit and talk about a whole range of subjects from family to philosophy. His name is Elias Ntshelewa Simela. Since he was much older than me, we had never spent much time together. I was amazed at how deep this man was. As I grow older, I have come to appreciate much of his wisdom even more.

When we were not engaged in hot political debates or protests of one kind or another, Friday nights were a time to hang out. There was a night club in Harare that even extended special admission privileges to college students. The music was good. The atmosphere was relaxed and very enjoyable. It was just a perfect place to relax and unload all the tension that one had built up during the week. Many of us took advantage of these free "therapeutic" sessions. Apart from this there was not much of a collective social life on campus. Every so often there was a dance. Otherwise people created their own social lives.

With all the wonderful food we ate, I gained a lot of weight. I joined a few of my colleagues as many evenings as possible to go to the gym and lift weights. I enjoyed doing this so much it became almost a ritual. Even though I kept most of the weight, it was more muscle than fat.

I also enjoyed a game of softball every now and then. There was not much of any sports activity on campus. Sometimes a few soccer enthusiasts organized a game. I would occasionally join in and try my old skills at it for the fun of it. Some people played rugby. But I had never learned that sport. It was not one of the sports played in the African schools. It was actually just another symbol of our divided society.

The majority of campus workers were black Africans. Since the university was located in Mt. Pleasant, deep inside the white suburbs, the workers did not live there. They were like migrant workers who were bused in each morning and bused out in the evening. It was sad to think that all these hard-working people were good enough to work there but not good enough to live in the area.

But such was the society all over the country. All towns had the white suburban community and the densely populated, miserable African townships. This was part of what the liberation struggle was all about and what all the demonstrations both on and off campus were all about. We were searching for justice and economic equality for all.

In July 1966, things reached a critical point. One night police came on campus and arrested dozens of students and college professors. Most of the professors arrested had come from abroad. They were from countries like Canada and Italy. We woke up to this chaos and an announcement that the college would be closed immediately. Everybody was to pack their bags and go home that day. There was no chance for the students to gather and protest in any way.

The whole idea was to have us disperse and thus prevent us from carrying out any more demonstrations. The demonstrations had galvanized the masses, even though they could not hold rallies or demonstrations themselves. The other sore point in the eyes of the government was that from our college pulpit we were able to let the outside world know what was going on. Getting rid of the agitators would stop the flow of news to the outside world.

The students that were arrested were sent to a detention camp. The professors were deported back to their countries. The outside world protested against these arrests, detentions, and deportations. Since the Smith regime was determined to keep the agitators away from the masses, they agreed to grant them one-way exit visas from the country. In other words, they were allowed to leave provided that they never returned to the country.

But this was the country of their birth. If Ian Smith and his government knew what tremendous opportunities they opened up for these people, they would never have done this. Some people left the country and went to study abroad. They have since returned as college professors and even top-level government ministers. You never know when opportunity will come knocking on your door. Sometimes it may come dressed in a police uniform.

I left the university that day not knowing what the future held in store for me. We had all been caught by surprise. My friend Kalayi Njini and I took the slow daytime train (*umbombela*) back to Bulawayo. It was as if we needed the time on the train to ponder our future. We did plenty of that but came up with nothing concrete.

Our options were somewhat limited by the uncertainty. We did not know if the university was going to open again. We did not know if the closure of the university was just a way to scatter us around so they could arrest us without creating a big hullaballoo that might ignite the whole country.

What were our chances of going abroad without any scholarships? None.

Should we look for jobs? Should we look for alternative career training? There really wasn't much else out there. This was the only university in the country. In fact, it was just about the only established university in Southern Africa outside of South Africa. We knew that there was no way that South Africa would take us after their brother Ian Smith had kicked us out.

The slow coal train huffed and puffed its way through large and small towns and villages. For once we were able to see these places, and somehow in between reflections about our situation, we admired the scenery. The train conductor called out the names of the towns as if he was taking attendance in primary school: Hartley ... Gatooma ... Queque ... Gwelo ... and finally Bulawayo.

There seemed to be a gazillion stops between the towns. In some of the towns the train stopped for long periods of time. We concluded that the train staff had gone for tea. It was very interesting to see the activity at each train station. People were getting on and off the train with all sorts of baggage. On the platform, men, women, and children hustled around selling every conceivable item, from boiled eggs, roasted and boiled corn, sweet rids (sugar cane with thin soft stems), and cooked fresh peanuts, to live chicken and homebrewed beer. My friend and I bought some homebrewed beer at Ntabazinduna in order to share it the traditional way. Before we drank it we poured some down to share with our ancestors and to ask them for guidance (*ukuthethela amadlozi*). Then we passed the container back and forth while we engaged in conversations about everything from A to Z as we admired the scenery at the same time.

You will recall that Kalayi and I had known each other since Standard 5 at Wanezi Mission. As it turned out, that was to be our last drink together for many years to come—twelve years to be exact. The train huffed and puffed through a few more stations, spewing out a thick cloud of smoke into the air. Finally the horn sounded, signaling its arrival at the Bulawayo station. Kalayi and I shook hands and went our separate ways. He went to his brother's house for a day or two. I decided to visit my brother who was teaching at Nernane Primary School.

This was a small school in a remote area beyond Tsholotsho. I did this for two reasons: one was to visit my brother, since I really had nothing else to do; the other was that I figured it was highly unlikely that anybody would track me down there if they were looking to arrest me. I spent two rather interesting weeks at Nernane, after which I went back to Bulawayo.

When I got back I found out that a lot of things had happened while I was at Nernane. The most interesting of these was that my friend Kalayi had left the country. There had been an underground train that took people across the border, much like the Harriet Tubman Underground Railroad. While I was happy for my friends, I felt depressed, wondering if I had missed a golden opportunity. On the other hand, I had no idea what would happen to these people.

I took the bus home to my parents in the countryside. There was still no news about the university. My parents were very disappointed that the university had closed. Were my dreams to be a doctor shattered forever? I did not know. They did not know either.

I sat in our living room with my father late one afternoon, and we talked until it got so dark we could not see each other. We were so involved in our discussion that neither of us realized how late it had become. We were talking about what my options were for the future. I wanted to leave the country to seek greener pastures abroad. However, there were no guarantees. There wasn't even an open pathway to the outside world. Everything would have to be done underground. This would put me in danger of being arrested or even shot.

My parents would also be harassed and possibly arrested if they did not reveal my whereabouts. If I did succeed in crossing the border there was no guarantee that I would be able to study what I wanted. Granted, my sister and her husband were already in Zambia. However, there were too many crocodiles and snakes in the Zambezi River for me to risk my life. Besides those creatures, Ian Smith's soldiers were lined up all along the border with their fingers on triggers. These were not pleasant prospects for a parent to ponder about their twenty-two-year-old son who had such a promising future.

But that afternoon the odds and obstacles facing me and my parents were huge. As hard as I pressed my desire to leave the country, I did not want to do it against my parents' wishes. My father was of the opinion that I should contact my sister and see if she could do something to open a path for me. He wanted to see if she could get me a place in school or a scholarship that would enable me to leave home, yet give my parents some peace of mind.

I explained to him that contacting my sister might actually backfire and put us all in danger. If such communication were intercepted by the authorities, no one knew what could happen. He understood that too but still thought it was the best option. We never came to any conclusion. In the midst of all this, word came that the university would open its doors again in September of 1966.

I returned to the university in September. My heart and mind were not there at all. I really did not want to go back, but I had little choice. Things were different. The place was lonely. I had not heard from my friends. I did attempt to contact my sister as carefully as I could. I did not get the response I wanted. As it turned out, she was also in transition. They were hoping to go to the United States of America if her husband received a scholarship.

*Chapter 7*

# Bulawayo and the City Council

⁂ ⁂ ⁂ ⁂ ⁂ ⁂

A
t the beginning of November 1966 I left the university and applied for a job with the Bulawayo City Council. I got a job as a clerk in the Makokoba Housing Office. My job was to receive and record rent money from tenants. There were also tenants whose rent was paid by their employer. These were done under what was called *transfer files*, which we recorded as well. This was something entirely new for me. It was different from anything that I had ever done before except for when I stood behind the counter at my father's butchery a couple of times. The most interesting part of the job was the opportunity to meet people from all walks of life.

Makokoba Township is the oldest township in Bulawayo. It is also the most popular. Most black people who ever lived in Bulawayo have roots of some sort in Makokoba. It may be that their father or brother lived there. They may have spent many evenings or Saturday afternoons at the Big Bar (beer garden). Youngsters may have spent afternoons at the recreational center.

Many may have come to what was for a long time the only people's market: Mkambo, which still stands today. You can generally find anything there, from a safety pin to the most sophisticated outfits, from dried caterpillars to fresh vegetables to the most potent herbs. It is indeed a lively place.

Many of the vendors came to our office to pay for their permits. They usually had stories to tell, which made the day go by very quickly. I enjoyed strolling through the market every now and then at lunchtime. It was fascinating to watch the wheeling and dealing that went on. There were some savvy old ladies who could sell the Brooklyn Bridge to anybody.

The Big Bar was right behind our office. That was the place to go to whenever we wanted to listen to fascinating stories over a half-gallon container of home brew. Here hard working factory workers stopped to quench their thirst. The beer was in half-gallon and one-gallon plastic containers. Huge tanks of beer stand above the cashier's stand. At the cashier's desk there is a machine with glass containers of premeasured volumes. When the customer asks for a half-gallon, the cashier spins the machine and it fills up the half-gallon container. Then the customer puts his or her container underneath the prefilled glass container and the white juice just pours out. This process was repeated hundreds of times a day.

The breweries probably brought in more money to the city treasury than any other department. Whenever the large tanks ran low they called the breweries for a refill. This was the normal procedure until somebody thought of plan B. Instead of calling the breweries for a refill, the cashiers opened the water taps and made their own refills. They figured that most people were drunk already. Several gallons of water would not make any difference in the taste and strength of the beer. So they sold the diluted beer and made a few bucks for themselves before calling the breweries. Many people got into big trouble over this scam.

Traditionally, whenever there was beer drinking, there would be barbequed meat. That tradition was not lost by the people in the cities.

Entrepreneurs seized the opportunity and brought the meat right into the beer gardens. The cow's intestines (*amathumbu*) and stomach (*ulusu*) were always the favorite parts. All the supermarkets and butcheries might run out of these cow parts, but the beer gardens always seemed to have them.

Practically every township has a beer garden, but the Big Bar has always been special. It is certainly not the cleanest, nor not the most spacious. There are other beer gardens that are commodious and that even have rocks within the premises where people can spread out and sit. The beer comes from the same breweries. However, the Big Bar has always had a special appeal.

At the office the end of the day was always rather tense. We had to balance our sheets and take the money to Mr. Sachs, a grumpy old man. Mr. Sachs shuffled around the office all day, but at the close of business, he sat in his office and looked over the rims of his eyeglasses. He mumbled something that I never understood and never found out what he said. As we handed him the money and our balance sheets, he went to work right away. He counted every penny that came in. Mr. Sachs never took anybody's word. I suppose years of experience taught him to do things his way.

Once all the money was counted and banked, it was time to go home.

The end of the month was agonizing for a lot of people. When I first got to the office I was puzzled by the increased level of activity in the security office. Then I got thoroughly confused when I saw a pile of handcuffs cleaned and set out on tables. It turned out that the security police went out and used handcuffs to lock doors to the flats when people failed to pay their rent. I thought it was the cruelest thing to do to anybody. I was told that many other ways had been tried and did not work.

This method surely seemed to work. I think finding a door locked with handcuffs would get anybody's attention. Usually people came in and alternative arrangements were made to pay the rent.

My coworkers were pleasant people. Mr. Mtali came from Malawi via Zambia. Even though he had spent most of his life in Matebeleland speaking Ndebele, a dialect of Zulu, he had a hard time pronouncing the words. He knew his job. However, many people had a hard time understanding him. It is true that some Ndebele words are very difficult to pronounce. Words like *xoxo* for frog, *qoqoda* for knock, *gxoba* for run over, and *gcina* for keep are not easy to pronounce unless you are a native speaker. But Mr. Mtali was fun to work with. He taught me the job and some Nyanja words as well. I learned quite a bit about Malawi and the culture of the Nyanja people talking to him.

Then there was Mr. Sibanda. He was a tall, rather imposing gentleman from Plumtree. As long as he had his cigarettes he did not bother anybody. There was no such thing as a smoke-free environment in those days. The most interesting thing about Mr. Sibanda was that he kept a tall bottle under his desk. In this bottle there was a concoction of all kinds of roots and things in water. He drank from this bottle every day and then he would refill it with water. This was home-brewed Viagra. I was tempted to try it.

Just looking at the mixture turned my stomach a little. I wanted to get a fresh bottle for myself, but he would not tell me what the ingredients were. I guess I will never know. I have since seen other mixtures for the same purpose. Some of these herbs are now in powder form. A teaspoon of this stuff in a cup of tea turns men into frisky cats. I guess that answers the question of why there is a population explosion in the country.

I worked in the Makokoba Housing Office for a few months. In March 1967 I returned to the University College of Rhodesia. Things had not changed much as far as the political climate in the country was concerned. There was a tremendous amount of frustration and very few outlets to release the tension.

The college was no longer the freedom patch that it had been before. There was a somberness in the atmosphere that had not been there before. I took four courses: botany, zoology, geology, and chemistry.

They were all interesting courses. If the atmosphere had been more conducive to studying, I would have enjoyed them.

In botany we spent a lot of time studying the forest and how the plants tend to differ in height depending upon their need for sunlight. We studied the Flora Zambesiaca, which went into great detail about the various types of leaves, grass, trees, and where they thrived. We spent a lot of time at the botanical gardens looking at preserved leaves and plants. Our professor was really into this stuff. But it was not exactly what I wanted to spend the rest of my life doing.

Zoology was much more appealing to me. Perhaps this had to do with my lifelong interest in medicine. We dissected a number of creatures, including a snake, which was probably the worst day of my life. You may recall that I am petrified of snakes. They had the nerve to bring a live one and put it in a glass container in the middle of our table. There was a dead one right in front of me to dissect. These were puff adders. They are short and fat with a brownish stripped skin. This was not a good day for me, but I had no choice. I survived it.

Dr. Bursell was conducting a very interesting experiment in the Zambezi valley to try to eradicate malaria. His theory was that one could take mosquitoes and breed them in such a way to eliminate their ability to carry malaria. Then one would take these inbred mosquitoes and release them in the Valley. They would breed with those in the wild. Hopefully, after a while the gene that enabled these mosquitoes to carry malaria would be bred out. Today we would call this genetic engineering, a term unheard of back then. On paper his theory was very exciting. It had the potential to save many lives around the world.

Dr. Bond, a superb professor, taught geology. He knew his rocks and fossils well. I had been around rocks all my life, but I found I knew nothing about them. This was an interesting course mainly because it was practical. Dr. Bond took us on field trips to such places as the Mazoe area where we saw rock formations that made the aging process seem real. We went to the Sinoa caves and saw pretty stalagmite formations.

We studied the various minerals found along the Great Dyke, which leads down to the diamond mines in South Africa.

We learned about the first class chrome found in Selukwe. This created a big problem between the United States and the United Nations in the late sixties. The United Nations had imposed economic sanctions on Rhodesia in 1965 because of its Unilateral Declaration of Independence. However, the US needed this fine chrome for its space projects. Otherwise the only other source was the Soviet Union. They would not go there for the chrome.

A special amendment was introduced in Congress to break the sanctions on this particular product. We also learned about the mineral used to make TV screens. It was mined along the Great Dyke. Because of the lack of facilities to refine the product, it was sold as raw material. When it came back as TV screens, no one could afford it. What a drain of Africa's natural resources!

Despite all this fascinating stuff, things were really not going well on campus. I had been assigned an advisor, as were all students. His name was Mr. Mitchell. He was a stocky white man whom I really never got to know, nor did I really want to. He told me at one of our sessions that I did not belong at the university. He told me that he could arrange for me to go to a technical college somewhere. I told him in no uncertain terms that I was not going to a technical school. I would go to the university no matter what he said. I don't think he liked my attitude.

Since graduating from Hamline University, I have never had the pleasure of meeting him. I actually considered mailing him a copy of my diploma. Such is life sometimes. I have learned to keep my eyes on the ball and never let the noise distract my attention.

At the end of 1967 I left Harare without completing the bachelor of science program. I went back to the Bulawayo City Council and applied for a job again. I got my old job back. I went back to the Makokoba Housing Office. Some of my coworkers were still there. However, I did not remain there very long. I was transferred from the Housing Department to the City Employment Expenses Department, called Vundu. The office was located at the Third Avenue extension. My duties included handling employee annual leaves, sick leave, and workers' compensation. It was all different.

One thing I missed was having direct contact with people as I had at the housing office. Here much of the work involved paperwork and signatures. I have never had to initial as many documents as I did then. I worked with several people in the office. Each of us had our own cubicle, so we could not interact much with each other. The man in charge of the office was Mr. Hendrickson. I found him to be too bossy and unfriendly. Given the political climate in the country, I did not expect anything different from him.

There was another gentleman named Mr. Savage. He did his thing, or was supposed to be doing his thing in his cubicle. However, he seemed to think that he was in charge of the office and everybody in the office. He was downright nasty.

Another colorful worker was Mr. Juba. He had seen it all. He knew his work. Mr. Juba was a middle-aged medium-built gentleman with a pleasant personality. I do not recall a day when he lost his temper despite all the abuse he took from his superiors. I was amazed one night when I went to a concert and found Mr. Juba conducting the choir. He was dynamite. Mr. Juba always had stories to tell. I was pleased, when I went back almost twenty years later, to find that he was still working for the same department. The difference was that the department had been moved to an ultramodern building. He was still as pleasant as he had been twenty years earlier.

Our office was conveniently located, within walking distance from the city center. There were several buses that stopped near the office that I could take to go home and several places nearby where one could go for lunch or for a drink. We had a whole hour for lunch. The office was closed during this time. Many people even went home to eat.

I generally had a standard lunch unless I went with someone or decided to go for a stroll in the city or the People's Market. I always had a banana, a meat pie, and a soda. When I go to Zimbabwe now I always make sure that I have a meat pie (*beefpatty*).

One day we went into the adjacent beer garden for a drink. We found a couple of gentlemen whom my coworker knew. We sat and shared a beer with them. A few minutes after we returned to work these gentlemen came into the office with somebody in handcuffs. First of all, I was rather shocked because I did not know that these people were undercover cops. I found out that the man had been arrested for selling marijuana. This was the first time in my life I heard of someone selling marijuana. It was also the first time that I saw someone being arrested for selling drugs. I had always known marijuana to be something that old people smoked from time to time. An old man in our village that we called Grandpa always had a small garden where he grew marijuana and tobacco. We helped him to cultivate his crop. None of us ever thought of even trying this thing, let alone selling it.

The undercover cops had come to use the telephone so that their station could send a car to pick them up. I don't know if I was just naïve or truly innocent.

I didn't return to the university in 1968. I had not heard from my friend Kalayi in a long time. Even though I was working and things were going well at the City Council, my mind was not at all settled. I kept myself busy with all sorts of activities and with friends and family. However, all the time I was looking for a way out of the country. I knew that was the only way that I could get a decent education and a career.

I joined a dance club that met on weekends and occasionally during the week where I learned to do the fox trot, waltz, tango, and quickstep, and enjoyed this very much.

I also joined a drama society. We practiced at McDonald Hall. The last play we did was about the crucifixion and death of Jesus. We did this during the Easter holiday in 1968. It was a lot of fun. I got to know a lot of interesting people like Reverend Deka and Mr. Mtsitsi.

I enjoyed life in Bulawayo. At one time I even thought it was the greatest city in the world. I once said that I did not want to live anywhere beyond a twenty-five-mile radius of Bulawayo.

I had a lot of friends in town. There was really never a dull moment. I would have had even more fun if I'd had a car. But even then, the city was not that big. So I got around very well by mass transit. There were buses, taxicabs, and the people's taxis (*imtshova*). These were the unofficial cars and vans that were privately owned and operated. It was often faster to get into one of these than to wait for a bus. It was also cheaper than calling a taxi. However, they were not the most glamorous means of transportation. Sometimes we literally sat on the tailgate of station wagons with legs hanging outside. The drivers were hardworking men who owned cars trying to make an extra buck to supplement their meager salaries.

I popped into *shabbeens* every now and then. These were the equivalent of social clubs in people's residences. Many people eventually made businesses out of these. These people bought drinks: beer and liquor in large quantities which they sold to clients who came around after the liquor stores and bars closed. Sometimes they provided musical entertainment. More often than not people just sat around and enjoyed the company of their friends.

Some *shabbeens* were more popular than others depending upon the *shabbeen* queen's style and attitude. In some cases they had cooked or roasted meat and other things to eat. As long as there was no violence, these places provided an avenue for people to relax.

There was no shortage of religious activity particularly on Saturdays and Sundays. This seems always to be the case where poverty, oppression, and despair abound. Religious melodies shared the airwaves with pop and jazz. There seemed to be an abundance of people in white clothes and some in khaki shirts and pants—the church uniform. People seemed to flock into these churches to find solace and comfort.

The country was going through tough economic and political times. Apart from its religious message, the Zion church taught self-reliance.

Its people were found turning scraps of metal into dishes, buckets, and other implements. They sold them on street corners and in the marketplaces.

Every now and then a popular music group came up from South Africa to perform a series of concerts. Places like the Stanley Hall or McDonald Hall (not the hamburger chain), Khwezi, White City Stadium, or Barbourfields were very popular venues for such activities. They kept people entertained.

At this time I did not have a car. I did not even know how to drive. I relied upon mass transit and friends. Fortunately, I was always able to get around town without too much trouble. The only time when I had trouble was when I wanted to go home to my parents in the countryside. I worked almost every Saturday morning until about noon. Therefore, I had to arrange for an afternoon departure on Saturday. Going home during the week was completely out of the question, even though the place was only about forty-five or fifty miles from town. The buses that transported people to the countryside generally left Bulawayo shortly after noon, which was inconvenient for me.

A trip on one of these countryside buses was always an adventure from beginning to end. The buses departed from a common terminal known as Renkini. Our bus line was called Magedleni, owned by the Dube brothers. They carried everything from the people to large bags of cornmeal, furniture, and building materials. Remember—many of the passengers were working men and women. Many went home probably only once a month or once every two months. These were generally family men and women who had homes in the countryside. This is why whenever they got a chance to visit their loved ones they brought everything that they could lay their hands on. All these buses had carrier racks on top. This is where the luggage was loaded. They generally did a good job of tying everything down so that nothing would be lost along the way.

The bus terminal was like a beehive on Saturdays and Sundays. There were hundreds, even thousands of travelers. They would be running in all directions trying to catch the right bus to their destination. These were often people like me who were coming straight from work. But since people were going to homes where there was generally a shortage of just about everything, they needed to buy lots of things. People from town were almost always expected to bring bread. Cream donuts were another favorite. At the bus terminal there were people selling all kinds of things ranging from candies to clothing—even blankets.

The noise that these merchants made to get people's attention was sometimes unbearable. This was one hell of a crazy place. Somehow, despite what often appeared overwhelming, people found each other, and found their way out of town and presumably reached their destinations.

For us the green, white, and red bus often pulled out around 1:00 p.m. The driver was usually a man by the name of Bhotha, a big man who was also one of the owners of the company. They whistled and blew horns to get the attention of the people milling around and to let would-be passengers know that the bus was leaving. Inside the bus there would be standing room only. But the police did not allow people to stand. Every passenger was required to have a seat. So the conductors would tell those passengers that had no seats to kneel down until the bus was out of town. The chance of being caught was less on country roads. Of course, if a passenger wanted to get home they would obey the conductor.

The fifty-mile journey easily took three to four hours, sometimes even more. Apart from the fact that the buses were very slow, they stopped at every village corner and every little store. At these stops people got off and hid behind bushes to relieve themselves. Sometimes they ran into the bottle store to buy beer. But the most time-consuming thing was getting people's luggage down from the rooftop carrier. Depending upon how many passengers were getting off, this process could take as long as half an hour. That's where all the hours went.

The good thing is that most people understood. After all, some of them had done this their whole lives. It was not a journey for the young and restless.

I lived with a cousin of mine, Mr. Elijah Msimanga. He was the same gentleman who had lived in a single room at Makokoba for many years. He had moved across the river to a development known as Sotshangane Flats in Nguboyenja where he occupied flat number 75. He had two bedrooms, a living room, a kitchen, and a bathroom. This was a major accomplishment for him. There was even electricity. One did not have to go outside to use the toilet. Even though the walls were bare bricks with no plaster or paint, the place was clean.

When his wife, MaNgwnya, was pregnant, she came to live with us so that she could be close to the hospital. For some reason my cousin decided to go out of town one weekend, and that is when his wife went into labor. Fortunately, my brother was there for the weekend.

She woke us up in the wee hours of the morning to tell us that it was time to get to the clinic. Remember, there were no telephones anywhere nearby in those days. The nearest telephone was at the police station. So my brother and I trotted to the police station to call for an ambulance. Neither one of us had any experience delivering babies. We were just praying and hoping that the baby would wait until she got to the hospital.

Things went well. The ambulance came and took her to a nearby clinic known as Mzilikazi. She delivered a healthy baby boy she named Nzuzo (a gift). There were a number of problems, though. My brother had to catch an early bus to get back to where he was teaching. There was absolutely no way to contact my cousin. The clinic where she delivered did not provide food except for some soft porridge. They certainly did not provide anything for the baby. She was allowed to stay only a day or two.

This was a Sunday morning when everything in town was closed. I knew absolutely nothing about babies. You can imagine what a state my mind was in. The only thing that I could think of was to go to my Rock of Gibraltar and steady source of wisdom and comfort: my parents. So I hopped on a bus and went to Longfield. There I explained the situation to them. My father gave me some money and told me to go to a lady at a certain store early in the morning. This lady would help me to buy all the things that the baby and mother would immediately need. I did exactly that.

Sure enough, the next morning I left the shop with all kinds of things, including a small tub to bathe the baby in. I arrived at the clinic looking like the proud father of a newborn baby. Thankfully, there was a happy ending to what had seemed like a major disaster. Nzuzo is now a grown man working for himself.

One day in March a friend of mine walked into my office. He looked depressed. This was a man I had known for more than ten years, during which I had never seen him without a smile on his face. Dan had given up his teaching post to go to the university to further his education. But something had gone wrong during the registration period and he was unable to start classes.

In that politically charged atmosphere it did not take much to derail your plans. In any case, we had to figure out something quickly. Dan's mind was so focused on furthering his education that he did not want to hear anything else. I asked him to go to one of the older gentlemen by the same name and wait for me there. When I left my office all three of us sat down and tried to figure out what his options were. Nothing seemed to make sense right away.

Dan and I went to my apartment and spent the next four days trying to find a way out. Luckily, we bumped into an elderly gentleman who had come from Botswana to sort out some family problems in Zimbabwe. This man had come across the border, as he had done all his life, without any travel documents. He was due to return on Sunday. This was now Friday. We made arrangements for Dan to travel with him to Botswana.

One problem was that Dan's luggage was too heavy to carry. We found another friend of ours, Stanley, who had proper travel documents for Botswana. Dan would leave his luggage with me. Once he was safely over the border he would send me a signal. Then I would get Stanley to take the luggage to him. This seemed like a perfect plan.

The next Saturday, we took the old man to a beer garden known as Minyela. There we shared beer with him and others. It was also a farewell party of sorts for Dan, except that I do not believe anyone else knew this besides me.

On Sunday morning we picked up the gentleman and headed for the train station. No documents were required to travel to Plumtree. I bought Dan a packet of Benson and Hedges cigarettes. With only the clothes he had on and a rabbit skin blanket over his shoulder, he boarded the train bound for Botswana. They would get off at Plumtree and walk the rest of the way, a long way across the border. The risk of being shot at by the border patrol and the ruggedness of the terrain did not deter Dan.

His mind was focused on a higher goal. The plan worked flawlessly. I received a coded message from Dan a few days later. According to the plan, I dispatched Stanley to Francistown with Dan's luggage. I did not hear from Dan for about three months. In June he called to tell me that he was leaving for Zambia the next day. He told me what to do and who to see when I got to Francistown. He knew that I was right behind him.

I did not know what had happened to Dan for nearly seven years. When he surfaced he was in Sofia, Bulgaria, attending school. Today he owns his own economic consulting company after obtaining a PhD in economics in Sweden. He has worked for the United Nations and still does consultations for them.

There is another story with a happy ending. My friend Kalayi, with whom I had traveled from Harare when the university closed in 1966, finally wrote me a letter. He had found his way to England and was studying at Leeds University. This was a great opportunity for him.

My sister and her husband had left Zambia. They were then students at the University of Minnesota in Minneapolis. They had met a young lady named Louise who was very interested in African affairs. They introduced her to me and we became pen pals. We discussed a wide range of subjects in our letters. She was also interested in knowing about my situation and future plans.

At that time my future plans were only what I wished and hoped I could do. I knew that there was nothing in Zimbabwe that would enable me to accomplish what I wanted. The only questions left were finding a country to go to and how to get there.

It is not easy to keep a secret. However, political developments in the country had taught us to be cautious. I knew I was going to leave the country. But I could not discuss this openly, even with my family, because it could have put them in trouble if the word ever leaked out.

In June I went home and spent a weekend with my parents. Somehow deep down I knew this was going to be my last weekend at home for a long time. I wish I had also known that this was going to be the last time I'd be with my father.

In the first week in July there was a holiday known as the Rhodes' and Founders' holiday. This was a commemoration of Cecil John Rhodes, after whom the country of Rhodesia was named. All government offices were closed. This was analogous to Independence Day in the United States.

The day before we closed our office, I prepared everything that I would have had to do when we came back after the holidays. I did not dare whisper even to a doornail what my plans were. My younger brother Oscar lived with me at the time. But he was not working. I asked him to go home and stay there for a few days. He did not know anything either. I did not want anyone to come and harass him about my whereabouts. The only person who knew the truth, and he also learned it the day before I left, was my cousin Elijah, with whom I shared the apartment. He was a seasoned politician who had seen just about everything. I was not worried about him. I knew he could take care of himself.

In fact, I think when the police came looking for me, he told them that I had gone to Harare for the weekend. He had not heard from me since. Harare is exactly the opposite direction from where I had actually gone.

I got up Saturday morning, July 6, 1968, and went to the train station much the same way as my friend Dan had done. With £40.00 (forty British pounds, then the equivalent of about $80 USD) in my pocket and hope in my heart, I said goodbye to Bulawayo and Zimbabwe.

I cannot describe my feelings that day. In many ways it was the hardest thing to do. Hopping onto that train I knew that I was leaving behind familiar surroundings and a certain job. By the way, I was due for a promotion that month. I was leaving behind my parents, brothers, and sisters without knowing when I was going to see them again. As it turned out, I would not ever see my father again. I was leaving behind my friends and the country I loved. Ahead of me there was nothing but uncertainty. I could not even be certain where I was going to be at the end of that day.

But there was that burning fire in me which was not going to let any obstacles or uncertainty stand in my way. Come hell or high water, I was going to find a way to realize my dreams. In my mind I had given myself ten years to go out and get a career. This feeling and resolve were so strong that they permeated every cell of my body. This insulated me from the sadness associated with leaving behind loved ones. Apart from the fact that I did not know where I would be at the end of that day, I had never gone in that direction before—by train or by bus.

I was caught up in taking in the scenery. I had heard of places like Fig Tree, Marula, and Plumtree. On that day I was actually passing through some of these places. The language seemed to be changing with each passing station. Whenever I had heard of places like Fig Tree and Plumtree, I always thought they were big towns. I was rather disappointed when I realized that they were nothing but a train station and a couple of stores.

However, there was an incredible amount of activity at Plumtree. This was the crossroads of southwestern Zimbabwe. People from Botswana, South Africa, and Namibia passed through here en route to their final destination—wherever that may have been.

No doubt the Zimbabwean police were also active in the town trying to weed out illegal immigrants and prevent illegal emigration.

I do not even remember if I ate anything that day. At the end of the day I was in Francistown. I asked several people for directions to the refugee camp. Dan had told me to go there. I had a little trouble because the people I asked spoke Tswana which I did not understand. They obviously understood "refugee camp." Somewhere between pointing and picking up bits and pieces of what they said in Tswana, I managed to get to the camp.

Another big problem arose immediately. I could not stay at the camp until I had been cleared as a refugee. I had arrived on a weekend, and no one was processed on the weekend. I met some Zimbabweans, Luke and Maphosa, who had been through the process. They advised me to find a place to hide until Monday. Otherwise, if I reported my presence in the country, I would be locked up in jail until Monday without anything happening. They helped me to find a place in the township. I made sure I stayed indoors until Monday morning. That Saturday and Sunday were among the longest two days of my life. My nerves were fried. Over a million scenarios went through my head about what might happen on Monday when I reported to the police station. The possibilities ranged from nothing to being bundled up and tossed back over the border between Botswana and Zimbabwe.

I could not have predicted what actually happened, but it was none of the above.

Dad, Mayine Dick Simela. Picture from
driver's license August 23,1958

Mom, Makobo Elizabeth Mabhena with
Ebbie Msimanga, Christmas 1971

Ernest Simela, Matopo Secondary school, 1960

Home sweet home
I grew up here
Nswazi, Esigodini

Homestead, I grew up here

My family 2008 (L-R) Sipho, Ernest, Veronica, Ashley

My sister, Grace Simela-Sibanda

My brother-in-law, Dr. Ronald Mswelaboya Sibanda

Nelson Hellem Ernest Oscar Meshack
Brothers

With my brothers: (L-R) Nelson, Hellem, Ernest, Oscar, Meshack

Mayine Dick Simela
Standing left with Friends
Salisbury, Rhodesia

Dad(left) with friends

Sipho

Ernest

Ashley

2008

with my sons ( L-R ) Sipho, Ernest, Ashley

Oscar Grace Margaret Thandi Ernest
Joshua (cousin ) Hellem Meshack
Brothers and Sisters

Family at The Homestead

Simela family cemetry
Mayine Dick Simela
buried here

Family cemetery (Mom& Dad buried here)

Quthe Ncube with oxen ready to plow the fields

Quthe ready to plow the fields

Form 2 Class
Matopo Secondary School
Ernest simela..3rd row right

Matopo Secondary Form 2 class 1961

Ernest Simela 1964
Fletcher High Schoo'

Ernest Matopo Secodary School 1961

Ernest Simela 1962
Bulawayo Star Phot

Ernest Star Photos Bulawayo

Matopo Secondary School Form 4 class 1963

Ernest, School Teacher. Nyumbane Primary, 1964

Louise Platt
Mineapolis. MN

Louise Platt, Lake of The Isles, Minneapolis, MN

Grace Sibanda & Ginny Knight
Minnesota

Grace ad Gene Knight, Minnesota

Ernest Simela 2008

Dr. Olaf Runquist
Chemistry Professor
Advisor 1968-1973
Hamline University
St.Paul, MN

Mrs. Runquist

with Dr.Olaf Runquist, my Chemistry
Professor,Hamline University,MN

Prof. Leon Khight, North Hennepin Community College, MN

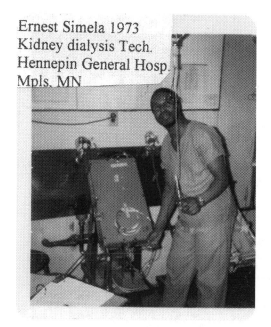

Ernest, Dialysis Technician, MN, 1973

Dr. Ronald Sibanda, Botswana

Ernest , New York

## Chapter 8

# Refugee Camp in Botswana

* * * * * *

Early on a Monday morning I went to the police camp in Francistown. This part I had not expected. No one had ever told me about it. As soon as I got there they simply took down my name and a few particulars. I was then immediately escorted to a small room with only one tiny window. I had always heard of people talking about looking out through a small window—in this case more like a small hole. I had never seen one. But on that day all my fears of prison life, based upon the stories I had heard, became real.

This was only the holding room. One other person was in there with me. I was so terrified that I do not recall holding any kind of conversation with my fellow prisoner. If there was any light in there, I did not see it. The only thing that I remember clearly was a bucket in the center of the room. This was our toilet. It seemed to me as if it had not been emptied for a few days. The room was about six feet square. The walls were solid cement bricks; they were not plastered or painted. The floor was solid concrete. There were no chairs or any kind of furniture. I believe the roof was made of corrugated iron, or it may have been asbestos. Whatever the roof was made of, it was high enough that one could not reach it without stepping on something. I suppose this was a precaution against attempts at suicide by hanging. One can only imagine the parade of people that had passed through that room over the years. The cast of characters would exhaust the adjectives in the English dictionary.

If I had not been as determined to go on and make something of myself, I think the temptation to say let me go would have been great. I could not think of a better way to break a person's resolve than putting them in this position. This was part of the process that the government used to weed out spies and common criminals from people who had genuine reasons for leaving the country. I was held in this room all day Monday, July 8, 1968. It was the longest day of my life.

I cannot even say that I had time to reflect upon anything because I was so traumatized by the whole thing. There I was in this dungeon, and not one person in my family even knew where I was. I had heard of solitary confinement, but this seemed to be simply cruel punishment. The worst part of the whole ordeal was the lack of communication. I was simply thrown into this room without any word as to what the next step was going to be or how long I was going to be there. It was hard to ask too many questions because I could just as easily have been bundled up and taken back to Zimbabwe. So it was hurry up and wait all day.

I couldn't even ask anybody because was no one was visible. It appeared as if the window or hole in the wall was deliberately located to look away from the prison offices. The only visible part of our surroundings was a very high barbed wire fence. I sat on the floor or stood up all day long. Any slight noise or movement at the door raised my hopes that perhaps someone had finally come for me. I heard many noises all day, real and imagined, but the door remained closed.

Thoughts about prison and the saying "Lock the door and throw away the key" crept into my mind every now and then. But I consoled myself by reminding myself that I had not committed any crime. It was simply a matter of time before this ordeal would be over.

Finally, at the end of the day I was let out of this holding cell and taken to the main prison where there were a large number of people. The prison cells were built around a courtyard where people were doing all kinds of things to keep themselves busy. I was led into a cell with about eight or ten people in it. This was another holding cell; none of the people there had been charged with any particular crime.

It was hard to communicate with the others since most people spoke in Tswana. At that time I did not understand any Tswana at all. I eventually learned some because I was in the country for about three months following my release from prison.

At the main jail, conditions were a little bit better. However, that bucket in the middle of the floor was still there. We were given a blanket to use at night. The floor was solid cement, which became very cold at night. There were no beds or chairs. The cell consisted of bare walls and a roof. There was only one window with heavy-duty burglar bars. There was no radio. TV did not even exist in the country at the time. There were no books or newspapers that I knew of.

The inmates were generally more relaxed, though I was probably more uptight than most of the other inmates. I didn't talk much because of the language problem, but I in the interests of self-preservation. I thought it was essential not to talk much because I did not know who was who in the prison population. Even though I understood perfectly why I was in that prison cell, there was something that just did not seem right about it. I could rationalize in my mind about why the government would want to put me in that cell, but that did not make it seem right.

I had known all my life that prison was a place for bad people. It was a place where you kept the scum of the earth. Prison was a dirty word. I did not think that any such descriptions came close to describing me. Therein lay my dilemma.

Every moment in this place was an education for me because just about everything was a new experience. The first rule was that one did not go into the cell with shoes or a belt on. All shoes came off and were left outside. All belts came off. Once again, I believe these were precautions against attempted suicide. But they were probably also precautions against prisoners trying to escape. It's no wonder then that I have strong feelings against today's young people walking around with pants hanging below their hips. In prison that happened because people were not allowed to wear belts. But I do not believe that young people should model their dress codes after prisoners. And so most of us were constantly pulling our pants up, which I found annoying and even humiliating.

We lined up for everything, or so it seemed to me. We lined up in the morning to take a shower and lined up to get our food rations served on metal plates. This was the only food available. There was no choice and no second serving. If you missed your turn, that was it for that meal. We lined up to get back into the cell. This was the most interesting ritual.

We were ordered to squat behind each other. At least two prison guards came around to do the counting. They touched each prisoner on the head with a stick as they counted out loud. If the count was correct, then we would be allowed to go into the cell. Once inside the cell for the night there was no chance of going out. If nature called, there was the bucket right in the middle of the floor. Thankfully, I do not recall anyone having diarrhea in our cell. Three days went by without me hearing anything from anybody. They were the longest three days of my life.

I have a lot of respect for President Nelson Mandela, who spent twenty-seven years in prison. I was convinced that prisons such as the one I was in were not meant for human habitation. I for one would do any and everything to avoid going there ever again.

On the third day, a Wednesday, I was taken back to police headquarters. After a brief interview I was given a temporary permit to stay at the refugee camp. I was told that after their investigation was complete I would be called back for a more thorough interview. This was a great relief.

They gave me documents and directions to the refugee camp, an old house named the White House by the refugees and located not far away, across the Shashi River near the airport. There were no buses or taxi cabs. Even if it had been far, I would have walked the distance rather than go back to that prison cell. I had no trouble finding the place, but I knew no one there.

However, the residents were very nice. There were people from Zimbabwe, Namibia, and South Africa. The camp was run by the United Nations Refugee Commission. The man in charge was a young gentleman by the name of Terrance. They told me how and where to find him. After walking around in circles I found his residence, and fortunately he was there. I presented my papers to him, and after looking them over, he welcomed me as a semi-official refugee —"semi" because I had not gone through the detailed interview at police headquarters. I was now entitled to receive whatever the other refugees received.

This was basically room and board. We were given blankets and assigned a bed at the White House. There were no sheets or towels, just two blankets. This was luxury compared to the hard cement floor at the prison cell. In southern Africa, July is the tail end of winter, so the nights can be very cold. Terry was also kind enough to give me the two-rand allowance for that week. Every week each refugee was given two rand (the equivalent of about $2.00 USD) for pocket money. This was enough to buy cigarettes for those who smoked, and perhaps a cold drink for others. Otherwise all refugees were given an allowance for food. This was not given to each individual refugee. Rather, each day two people were assigned to prepare meals. They were given the money to buy whatever was necessary to prepare meals for the day for everybody. I do not recall how the menu was arrived at or how much was given for the day. However, the system worked well. We seemed to get something to eat every day. Everyone chipped in, and the place was kept relatively clean.

There were a few more activities here than at the prison. Among the most valuable activities was the tutoring, which was directed mostly at Namibians who did not speak English. These were grown men. There were no women or children at the refugee camp. These people had either learned Afrikaans in school, or they knew only their native language. I quickly joined the English tutoring group. This kept me busy and kept my mind off thinking about my own situation.

We also started a dance club for recreation. In the afternoons we cleared some space and learned how to dance. Some refugees who lived in the township also joined in these activities. We got to be a large family.

We came from different backgrounds and different countries. However, we shared one common desire. We all wanted opportunities that we could not get in our homelands because of racial discrimination. All our homelands—Zimbabwe, Namibia, and South Africa—were struggling to achieve majority rule. That yearning for freedom came out clearly when we sang the national anthem "Nkosi Sikeleli Africa," which was somewhat universally known in Southern Africa. It was translated into different languages—Zulu, Sotho, Ndebele, Shona, and others. The tune is the same, so it was easy for all of us to sing it.

The song says "God bless Africa." But at the time the most important part was where the song says "Hear our prayers." The sense of hope was incredibly important at a time when it appeared as if white rule would never come to an end, which in turn meant that some of us would never return to see our loved ones again. Singing this song helped to keep hope alive.

On Monday mornings we were all required to go to the police camp for roll call. This was just a way of keeping track of who was still in the country and who was still in the vicinity of Francistown. The police camp also became a place where one got to meet other refugees. The rest of the day we spent doing whatever we wanted to do except when it was our turn to cook.

In 1968 Francistown was a very small town. It basically consisted of one street along the railroad station. There were two small hotels: the Grand Hotel and the Tati Hotel. In between there were a couple of stores: a clothing store and a general dealer. At the other end was a bakery. There wasn't much else as far as the shopping area was concerned.

Across the street was the train station. This railroad ran all the way from Zambia and Harare to Capetown, South Africa. So there was not much window shopping that one could do. Besides, we had no money to buy anything even if we wanted to.

Our favorite place was the Tati Hotel. We generally gathered there after the visit to the police station to share stories and perhaps have a drink. Every now and then there were people from home or from South Africa who were traveling on business. They would buy us a drink or two.

The Grand Hotel was patronized mostly by white people. Even though Botswana was now an independent country, it was still plagued by old habits. After all, the country's independence was in its infancy. To the north of the shopping area there was a hospital, the only one in town. It apparently provided excellent service. People were happy with it. In the same direction were the police headquarters and other government offices. To the west of the town, on the other side of the railroad tracks, was the Shashi River. During the time that I was there it was dry. There was nothing but sand all along the riverbed. African townships spread out across the river like mushrooms in the rainy season. There were sounds of music everywhere. Somewhere in these townships, off toward the northwest, was our White House.

In retrospect, it was probably not the best location for a refugee camp given the brutality of the regimes we had left behind. Indeed, there were bombings of refugee camps reported over the years.

We were well received by the people of Botswana. We were invited into their homes. We shared meals with them. We were invited to their parties and visited their *shabbeens*. I found them to be very pleasant people. While I tutored my fellow refugees who were trying to learn English, I had my own tutors. I gathered little children from the neighboring houses and asked them to teach me Tswana. They were the best teachers that I could have had. I had a lot of fun learning. I think they enjoyed teaching me too.

After three months in Francistown I understood and spoke a substantial amount of Tswana. I had no textbooks to read. Fortunately for me, they didn't give me any examinations to write. I found Tswana relatively easy to speak. But I was and still am totally baffled by the spelling of the words that are so easy to pronounce. As a result I never attempted to read or write it. It's a beautiful language. The sounds of the words when spoken well are musical.

While I was there I was also struck by another thing about the Tswana people: they are unusually nonviolent. There was a lot of drinking and partying going on, but I never heard of any arguments or fights nor of any police coming to break up a party or altercation of any kind. There were certainly no shootings or violent deaths reported in the three months that I spent in Francistown.

Botswana had recently won its independence from Great Britain. People were still celebrating their independence. There was very little political activity visible to the public except for a few rallies held by the opposition party led by Mr. Phillip Matante. This was a far cry from the political tension that I had left behind in Zimbabwe. There were no arrests and no detention of people. There were no soldiers crisscrossing the city and the country. People were not afraid to gather in public.

After several weeks at the refugee camp I was finally called back to police headquarters. This was a little unnerving because there was no way for me to know whether my status as a refugee had been approved. It was a moment when I could have been bundled up and sent back across the border if my story didn't check out. I went before the committee whose composition I do not really recall. Despite all the assurances from my fellow refugees that this was simply a formality, I was still a little nervous. A lot of things went through my head.

The most disturbing was the thought of being tossed back in that prison cell. I imagined a scenario where this committee told me that there was a new procedure whereby they sent people back to prison pending final approval. But as it turned out, there was nothing to be afraid of. They simply asked a few questions. Most of the questions had to do with what my future plans were: How long did I anticipate my stay in the country to be? How did I plan to accomplish what I hoped to do to gain my exit? Did I have any relatives in the country that I could stay with?

I thought these were fair and legitimate questions. The country did not want to be burdened by refugees, especially at this early stage of its independence. And so I was granted full status as a refugee. I do not recall if there was a time limit on the permit. The one stipulation was that I report to police headquarters every Monday morning and stay out of trouble, which I was already doing.

I assured them that they could expect no trouble from me and thanked them for their hospitality. Needless to say I left that office relieved and a very happy man.

Now I could pursue my plans without any fear. That is not to say I had not been working very hard to find a way out of Botswana to further my education. I had written to my sister Grace and her husband Ronald, who were then at the University of Minnesota in the USA. I told them that I had left Zimbabwe. I was now at this refugee camp and had no idea where I was going next.

In July 1968, I also wrote a letter to my pen pal Louise which said pretty much the same thing, but I also told her what I hoped to accomplish. I wrote, "Where my intelligence fails me, my determination will carry me through." Louise kept this letter. When I graduated from medical school in 1977, I invited Louise to my graduation. There she presented me with a copy of that letter.

Among my many other attempts to find a way out of Botswana were applications for scholarships. I applied to the British Commonwealth Scholarship program. In this way I hoped to go to a country like the UK, New Zealand, Australia, or anywhere, as long as I could get an education.

When I was in high school I had made applications to the United Nations for a scholarship to study medicine abroad. Two prospective countries that seemed promising were India and Romania. I figured that it would not hurt to try them again. My situation had changed drastically. I had completed high school with good grades. I had also done some studies beyond high school. Finally, I was in this desperate situation. I took my case up with our resident United Nations representative, Terry, who was in charge of the camp. Of course he told me that the only thing that I could do was to apply, so I made a trip to Gaborone, the capital city of Botswana. There I went to the British High Commission and the American embassy to appeal in person. They were all very understanding. But I got the same answer, which was that I should apply to the appropriate agencies or departments.

This was the first time that I had gone this far South. Gaborone is very close to the South African border. It was an overnight journey by train from Francistown. We passed through such towns as Palapye and Mahalapye, which I had heard of in my geography lessons. It was exciting to actually see places that had seemed so far when we read about them.

The train arrived in Gaborone early in the morning, before any offices opened, so I had some time to explore the city. I was surprised to learn what a small town it was. First I saw the train station and big government buildings, including the house of Parliament. There was a small shopping area where there was a bank and both the American embassy and the British High Commission. The main gathering spot was the President Hotel, also located in the vicinity of the shopping center. The rest of the town seemed to be an expanse of residential areas.

I was amazed when I returned to Gaborone nine years later, in 1977. The city had grown to an incredible metropolis. Huge five-star hotels like the Holiday Inn overshadowed the old Grand President Hotel. It was like being in an entirely new city. Nevertheless, I found the same small Fish-n-Chips store where I had bought my breakfast in 1968 and made it a point to buy some fish and chips.

Even though I didn't get much from the places that I visited, I felt like the contacts were important. As it turned out, when I eventually had to apply for my British passport and an American visa, I dealt with the same people that I talked to on this trip.

I returned to Francistown after that one day in the capital. Once again I took the overnight train. Somehow it appeared as if there were more trains traveling by night than during the day. I would have thought that it would be safer to travel by day. Cattle ranching is popular in Botswana, and there are also a lot of goats crossing the roads. Therefore, when traveling by night one is likely to come across some of these animals, which can be dangerous.

The trip itself was uneventful, although I was rather amazed at the number of people catching the train in the wee hours of the night, some getting on the train in places that seemed to be in the middle of nowhere. But a large part of the rural areas did not have electricity yet. Even though there may have been large villages near the train station, there would be no lights to indicate the size of the town or village.

I am not sure which came first—the railroad or the development, but the land along the railroad was the most developed and populated parts of the country. Another large part of the country is desert. I wished that I had had the means and freedom to travel around to some of these outlying areas. I had heard that there were some beautiful tourist places around. I also wanted to visit some areas where the Bushmen lived. We read all kinds of history about the Bushmen. I had seen Bushman paintings in Zimbabwe. But all this was still academic because I had never actually seen the people described as Bushmen. I never got a chance to do any of that. I was back in Francistown the next morning. There was not much to do except to report that I was back in town.

One other avenue that I was exploring in my quest for a way out of Botswana was the political party that I was affiliated with, Zimbabwe African Peoples Union (ZAPU), then headquartered in exile in Zambia. Many people had gone abroad through the party and its contacts. People had gone to various parts of the world for a variety of reasons. Some had gone for technical training in fields ranging from secretarial work to engineering. Others were in colleges and universities to earn academic degrees in all sorts of subjects: history, English, math, and science. For some of these people the goal was to teach.

The party had to get assistance whenever and wherever it was available. Its ultimate goal was to prepare for eventual majority rule. When the country became independent, it would need all kinds of skills and manpower. However, the road to majority rule was unclear and certainly uncharted. At that point in time it seemed obvious that independence would come only through a violent struggle.

The party initiated guerilla training. This meant that the options for a young man going through the party ranged anywhere from an academic assignment to military training. I kept all options open.

Botswana is generally a dry country. August of 1968 was especially dry and hot. I had not brought any shorts with me, so I wound up having to buy a pair in Francistown. That month was also figuratively dry as far as any developments in my situation were concerned. I did not get anything from the Commonwealth Scholarship Program. That had been my best hope.

There wasn't much coming out of Zambia either. So I just kept busy and took each day as it came. In the early mornings we were always aroused by the big planes carrying migrant workers from places like Zambia and Malawi on their way to the gold and diamond mines in South Africa. People called them *wenela* planes. To this day I do not know what that means. In any case, there were more of these planes landing and departing from the airport in Francistown than any other types of planes.

Every day I hoped and prayed that one day I would go to that airport to board a plane taking me to some destination where I would further my education. The hot days of August came and went. There were no positive developments. I had written to just about everybody and to every agency that I could think of.

Finally, in early September I got a letter from my sister and brother-in-law in Minnesota. They told me that they were working on a way to get me to the US. They told me to hold on because things were promising. I was elated. This was the best news that I had heard in two months.

Meanwhile, a South African music group led by Reggie Msomi took the town by storm. They performed for two nights. They had just finished a tour of Zimbabwe. This group was excellent. There was music everywhere in town. I got a chance to meet Reggie Msomi—an amiable fellow with a great sense of humor. They left town shortly after their last performance. It had been a memorable night of music and dance. I was still high from the news about the possibility of going to the States.

The following week the circus came into town. This was my first visit to a circus ever. I was speechless. It was the first time that I had seen a live elephant and a live tiger—in fact, the first time that I had come so close to most of the animals that they had. But to see these wild animals perform at the command of a human being was just incredible. I thought the whole show was wonderful.

My fingers were still crossed when I received another letter together with some documents from the US. My hands were literally shaking as I opened it. I think my heart may have skipped a couple of beats as well. The very fact that there were documents seemed to me to be a good sign, even though I did not know what they were. There was a cover letter explaining what they were. I almost started celebrating when I saw the word *college* even before I read anything else. This was the real thing. I had been accepted at North Hennepin Junior College in Minnesota. It did not matter that I did not understand the difference between a university, college, and junior college. The important thing was that I was finally on my way out of the refugee camp, out of Botswana, and on to some place to further my education.

I finally calmed down enough to read the whole letter and look over all the documents. The letter explained the documents and the steps that I needed to take immediately. The most important document was a long piece of paper labeled I-20 Form. This was the document issued by the accepting college. It was this document that would enable me to apply for a student visa, without which I was not going anywhere. I did not know it at the time, but came to find out later that a complete stranger to me had been most helpful. A gentleman with a big heart by the name of Leon Knight had been instrumental in helping me to gain acceptance at North Hennepin Junior College.

Once everything was in order, the I-20 Form was issued. I shall forever be grateful to Leon and Ginny Knight. I came to know them well over the years that I spent in Minnesota. But before the I-20 Form could be issued, there was one crucial step left. The college had to be assured that there was adequate financial support for the student to whom this form was issued.

Once again my dear sister, Grace, her incredible husband, Ronald, and my compassionate pen-pal Louise stepped in. They came up with not just the tuition guarantee, but with the guarantee of room and board and a plane ticket. I was humbled when I read the letters, saw the documents, and realized what these people had done on my behalf. It made me believe in humanity in a way that I had never done before. Who would have thought that a little shepherd in a the remote village of Longfield in Zimbabwe would find so much help in the Land of Ten Thousand Lakes—Minnesota?

Even if I had thrown a dart at a map of the world with my eyes wide open I doubt seriously that I would have hit the Twin Cities. But there it was; perfect strangers to me and to each other had come together and tossed a lifeline that rescued me from a desperate situation. I caught the rope and was determined to hold on tight.

I followed all the instructions to a T. The first thing that I needed was a passport. I had to go back to Gaborone to the British High Commissioner for that. Once I got the passport I could then go to the American embassy to apply for a visa. I went over the documents again to make sure that everything was in order and that I understood every step.

After I was certain that all the documents were in order, I went to Terry, the UN representative in charge of the camp. I explained to him what steps I needed to take in order to go to the US. He was most accommodating. He even gave me an allowance for the train ticket to Gaborone. Because this trip was likely to take more than one day, I needed permission. I would also need to report to the police camp there since that day was going to be a Monday. At this point I did not care who I reported to. All I wanted was clearance to leave.

Once again I boarded the coal train bound for Gaborone. This time I took the day train because I wanted to enjoy the scenery. It was possible that I would not be taking that train again. As it has turned out, I have not been on that train ever since.

The train was crowded, but I managed to find a window seat that was just perfect for me. With a thick cloud of smoke shooting into the air and a whistle blowing, the train started the long journey to the capital. The brown and yellow cars slowly swayed from side to side as the train picked up speed. There was not much to see because the land was dry. Every now and then one saw a few goats picking dry leaves off the bushes and cattle wandering aimlessly in search of grass.

At the train stations there were people selling everything from boiled eggs to wood carvings. I enjoyed listening to the musical tones of the Tswana language between people saying their goodbyes and others hawking their wares. In between the train stations I listened to the staccato sounds of the metal train wheels on the iron rails interrupted by the joints. The steady, repetitive nature of the sound was almost hypnotic, but I resisted the temptation to sleep. I did not want to miss anything. Finally the train pulled into Gaborone station. I had been here before.

Terry had arranged for me to spend a night with someone he knew. He had given me directions to his house. As soon as I got off the train I made my way there. The gentleman was very understanding. He turned out to have been a policeman, which made me a little uncomfortable. But I had come to trust Terry and knew that he was not likely to jeopardize my future in any way. The gentleman was a gracious host.

The next morning, after breakfast, he accompanied me to the police camp so that I could report my presence in Gaborone, as instructed. That was easy and painless. With that out of the way, my real mission started.

I went to the British High Commission and applied for a passport, where I received excellent assistance. They understood the need for me to get a passport as quickly as possible so that I could move to the next step. The fact that they remembered me from a previous visit was helpful. I was not just someone coming off the street and applying for a passport. It took a few hours for me to get clearance for a passport. In the meantime, they had given me documents indicating that I was going to get my passport. So with that I was able to go to the American embassy to initiate my visa application. I suspect that someone may even have called the American embassy to let them know that I was coming and that they were working on my passport. Everything worked out flawlessly. I got all my documents without any hitch.

The question of the plane ticket had been addressed in the accompanying letter. I was supposed to fly from Botswana and spend a night in Zambia. Someone advised me to get a transit visa from the Zambian High Commission. So I went to their office as well. I was very lucky to find a secretary that was actually from Zimbabwe. She made life easy for me—maybe too easy. I got a transit visa in the form of a document. It was not stamped in my passport. For me this was good enough. It was an official government document issued by a legitimate government agency. Now I was all set to go to America, except that I did not yet have a ticket. My ticket was booked on Pan American Airlines. It was supposed to arrive in Gaborone by air from Johannesburg in South Africa. The ticket did not arrive when it should have come. I called the Pan Am offices in Johannesburg. They knew about my ticket. But whoever had written it either needed some basic lessons in geography or was trying to do something funny—we did not know which. My ticket had been routed to take me from Botswana back into Zimbabwe, the country that I had just left three months earlier to be a refugee in Francistown. I thought that would have been a smart thing to tell customs in Harare.

After a heated exchange with the Pan Am agents they agreed to rewrite my ticket correctly and give it to the captain of the next flight to Francistown. With that assurance my mission in Gaborone was essentially complete. All that was left was for me was to go back to Francistown and pack my bags. I was ecstatic.

That night I caught the train back to Francistown. I do not remember much about this train ride. I suppose all I was thinking about was life in the US. I had a lot to look forward to.

Even though I was just about to take my first airplane ride ever, it was the least of my concerns. Some people have reservations about flying. But even though I had never done it, my focus was on getting down to the business of studying and not on how I was getting there.

There was nothing unusual about the trip back to Francistown. It was another night ride with not much to see. I went back to the White House. My fellow refugees were happy for me. However, there was some sadness in their eyes. Some of these men had been there for months before I arrived. Now only three months later I had the opportunity to go overseas to study. As soon as I arrived I went to see Terry. I explained to him what I had accomplished and what was missing. I was not sure what date I was actually going to be leaving but it would be quite soon. For the time being all I could do was to hurry up and wait for my ticket.

I started saying my goodbyes to the local people that I had come to know. I gathered the children that had taught me how to speak Tswana. I told them that I was going to be leaving soon. I thanked them for having been such good teachers. There was something about leaving them that made me sad. I do not know what it was, but in retrospect, it was probably the pediatrician emerging in me. They seemed sad too. They wanted to know where I was going. But they seemed more excited about the fact that I was going to travel by plane. It was an indication that I was going to some place very far.

The butcher, Jack, was an amiable fellow with a bald head. We had always bought our meat from him for the meals at the camp. When it was my last turn to cook, I went there to buy meat as usual. I told him that it was probably going to be the last time that I came to shop. I told him I was going to America. He stopped what he was doing for a moment, and then said, "Good for you, young man." Then he said jokingly, "Send me some of that snow and ice. I can use it to keep my meat fresh."

I am sure their electric bills were very high. They had a small freezer where they kept the meat that was left over from the day's kill. I guess I had an interest in this business because butchering had been my father's line of work too. I went back to the camp and cooked a delicious beef stew with vegetables. I wanted to make it special, as it was going to be the last time that I cooked. We had cornmeal porridge and beef stew with vegetables. It was delicious. Everybody was happy.

Some of the residents teased me about cooking for the rest of the days that I was going to be there. They knew that that was not going to happen. I have never been very fond of the kitchen. However, those last days I made every activity a celebration of some kind.

For example, usually at mealtimes people would dish out and then go and sit in small groups or alone somewhere. This time everybody hung around and shared the moment of joy. I suppose they were hoping to get some ideas that would help them too. Everybody was always searching for a way out of the refugee camp. Going to college somewhere may not seem like a big deal. However, among the refugees were men who had left their families behind in search of freedom and a better life for themselves; for those left behind, going off to college took on a whole different meaning. I savored every moment and prayed to God to give me strength to seize the opportunity with every bit of strength in my body.

When I left Gaborone to return to Francistown, I did not actually have the passport or the American visa in hand. I had documents and assurances that those documents would be issued. I was uncertain of the timeframe that they were working with. However, for me it was important to get the documents and travel in time to start school at the beginning of the next semester. I worked very closely with Terry, the UN representative in Botswana. The arrangement had been that once the British High Commission issued my passport, it would be sent to the American embassy for them to stamp my visa in it. The completed documents would then be forwarded to me.

Terry kept in touch with everybody concerned. My passport was actually issued on September 13, 1968. It was apparently forwarded to the American embassy accordingly. They, in turn, issued me a student visa on September 18. There was still a holdup on my ticket. However, knowing that the most important documents had been issued I was not terribly worried. I was upset with the Pan American Airways people for not processing my ticket promptly and properly. My documents were sent to me by registered mail. Everything was in order except for the ticket.

I finally got confirmation that I was booked on a flight that would leave Francistown on September 25. The flight originated in Johannesburg and made connections in Gaborone. My ticket was going to be on that flight somehow. I was going to get it at the airport. That was rather scary because I could not be absolutely certain that the ticket would be there. I do not even remember if I slept at all the night before.

I wanted to take everything that I could carry from Africa. I knew I would not be coming this way again for a long time. I would certainly miss the motherland, so I wanted mementos that I could hold on to for all the years I would be gone. There was no question in my mind that I would return to Africa someday. I don't know how I came up with the figure of ten years, but that is how much time I gave myself. I prepared myself mentally to be away for at least ten years.

During that time I would go to school and get a career. I put together as many addresses as I could get ahold of. I would write to all my friends and relatives and tell them about my experiences in the New World. I would have liked to take my favorite foods, like sour milk—*amasi*, as we called it—mixed with fresh corn bread or ground sorghum; or corn cooked with melons (*umxhanxa*); and a whole variety of wild fruits. However, those who had traveled out of Africa told me that I could not do that. It was not allowed.

So I resorted to collecting whatever papers and books I had. Every cell in my body was tingling with anticipation of what surprises, excitement, and expectations lay ahead. My whole life and body were literally going to be transplanted somewhere across the vast Atlantic Ocean. I had looked to the West and imagined life at the end of the rainbow. No one had ever come back and described the village that lay at the end of the rainbow. However, it was hard to imagine anything else but a place as beautiful as the colors of the rainbow itself. In any case, nothing could be worse or more desperate than life at the refugee camp.

## Chapter 9

# The Long Journey to the USA

● ● ● ● ● ●

The big day finally came: September 25, 1968. That was the day when my journey across the ocean began. At the end of this journey I would find the end of the rainbow.

Terry came to the refugee camp at noon and found me burning some papers. He asked me if I was burning incense or speaking to my ancestors, asking them to clear the way for me. I told him that he was absolutely correct. We laughed. But it was true that I had turned my thoughts to thank every authority that I could think of who had helped me to get this far. I prayed that they would not fail me now.

My bag was already packed and ready to go. I said goodbye to my fellow refugees. There were no visible tears rolling down anybody's cheeks only because that was not considered manly. But there were certainly watery eyes. I had shared an unusual life with these otherwise perfect strangers. But because we had so much in common and shared a common desire, we had become brothers.

The watery eyes were tears of joy that one of us had found an escape route. That meant there was hope for those left behind.

I made my very first trip to the airport. This was not a sightseeing trip. I was the passenger. It is impossible to describe my feelings at that moment. I was certainly excited about the prospects but nervous about the possibility of things going wrong. At the airport we were met by a Mr. DaCosta, who was a native of the island of Jamaica traveling on a mission for the United Nations. This was exciting because I was already being introduced to the international community.

I had read about Jamaica, the beautiful resort island. This was the first time that I was actually meeting someone from there. Mr. DaCosta had my ticket to fly. I could have kissed his feet when he told me this. Now I was really ready to go. I had my passport, my visa, and my ticket.

We checked in at the ticket counter. There were no glitches. My journey was to take me from Francistown in Botswana to Lusaka in Zambia. We would spend the night there. On the twenty-sixth of September we would fly to Ndola, another town in Zambia. All this time we would be flying British Overseas Airways Corporation (BOAC), which no longer exists. From Ndola we were going to fly to Kampala in Uganda and then on to London, where I was going to spend another night. Finally, on September 27, 1968, I would fly from London to New York to Minneapolis, Minnesota. I think I must have pinched myself to make sure that this was really me. This was exciting stuff. I had never in my wildest dreams thought I would be making such a long journey in such a short time.

But yes, it was the real thing. I said goodbye to Terry and thanked him for everything that he had done for me over the three months I had been at the refugee camp. He had always been a gentleman—friendly, supportive, and very helpful. I told him how grateful all the other refugees were to have someone so understanding at that trying and difficult time in their lives. I promised to write to him and tell him about my journey.

With the bright African sun and oppressive September heat beating down on the tarmac, we walked to the plane. Mr. DaCosta had become my travel partner and newfound friend. This was a walk to be remembered. As far as I was concerned, once I made it past customs and the immigration officers, I was already in the land of freedom. Those last few steps to the plane were like the steps across the Red Sea in biblical times. Climbing up the steps into the plane was like climbing Jacob's ladder. At the top of the steps I turned and waved to Terry and the small crowd below. This was it. I had found my wings to fly.

I was already in a different world. For once a white woman, the airline stewardess, was going to serve me with all the courtesy that she could muster. One of them showed me my seat and helped me with my hand luggage. Once I sat down I had to figure out how to fasten the seatbelt, which turned out to be not very difficult. I thought that was cool.

I sat there like a seasoned traveler. However, inside of me there were butterflies. I wondered what it would feel like when the plane took off. I had heard of people being sick. I hoped that this would not happen to me, because for one thing I did not want to be embarrassed; but I also had a long journey by air ahead of me. The stewardess walked up and down the aisle passing candy. I had missed this bit about flying. No one had passed candy around when I traveled by train or by bus. So I thought this was a tradition peculiar to flying. At this point I was not prepared to reveal my ignorance by asking too many questions.

Fortunately, there were other people for whom this was a new experience too. A portly gentleman sitting a couple of rows ahead of me was brave enough to ask what the candy was for. He was told to eat it when the plane took off. It would help with the pressure in his ears. This was good enough for him and for me too, even though I could not for the life of me figure out what the lady meant by pressure in the ears.

Finally, they closed the doors and wheeled the steps away. A voice came over the speakers instructing the passengers to pay attention to the stewardess standing in the aisle. They were about to demonstrate the safety procedures. I hung on to every word and watched every action. After all, I figured that this could mean the difference between life and death. When they were done we were ready to go.

The moment of excitement had come. This was a decent-size plane. It picked up speed as it taxied down the runway. Within a very short time it seemed to be going one hundred miles per hour and the front part of the plane lifted straight up. I ate my candy and swallowed as fast as I could. We were airborne. Everything below us got smaller and smaller as we climbed up to cruising altitude. This was cool. I was not sick and I was not afraid. If anything, I was enjoying it.

This was a lunchtime flight. So once we reached cruising altitude they served lunch. I thought that was special treatment. Even though I had eaten my lunch at the camp, I was not about to miss this one. The food looked delicious. I don't recall exactly what was on the menu, but whatever it was it looked good. No sooner had we started eating than a voice from the cockpit came over the speakers instructing us to fasten our seatbelts. The next few minutes were terrifying to say the least. Dishes were flying all over the place. I thought for a moment that this was it. We had run into turbulence somewhere over the Caprivi Strip area. However, the pilot seemed to be in control the whole time. But for someone flying for the first time, this was not a happy experience. Thankfully, it was not a long flight. We landed safely in Lusaka, Zambia. The bumpy flight was the topic of conversation for many passengers.

Mr. DaCosta introduced me to a fellow refugee from South Africa. He had been at the refugee camp in Gaborone. Like me, he too had found an escape route. He was flying to London to study at Oxford University. I was very impressed because I had known for years that Oxford is a prestigious university. I had never actually met any students from there.

We all made our way toward the immigration officers. While waiting in line we discussed the arrangements for the night. We had reservations at a hotel. My South African colleague had made the same arrangements that I had made while I was in Gaborone. He had a travel document issued by the United Nations because South Africa was not a colony of Britain as Zimbabwe was. I had a British passport because technically I was a British subject. He also had obtained a transit visa at the Zambian embassy in Gaborone just like me. When we got to the immigration officer we hit a roadblock. He called us stateless people and showed us a bench in a corner somewhere to sit. Mr. DaCosta was allowed to proceed.

After what seemed an eternity, this absolutely ruthless man called us. He told us that our transit visas were useless documents that had not been approved. He threatened to send us to prison pending clearance. Both of us were frightened and discouraged. It seemed as if this man had the authority to derail our trips and lock us up. But because jail was one place neither one of us wanted to see again, we protested rather vigorously. We had not stolen or bought those transit visas. As far as we were concerned they were official documents issued by the Zambian government agency. He made phone calls to Livingstone, a town near the border between Zambia and Botswana. We were not privy to the exchanges that took place.

After a couple of hours of detention he finally let us go. It was not clear to us what the terms of our release were, because he sent us out with a young man as an escort. Once outside, as I recall, we gave this young fellow a couple of rand and he gave us our travel documents and vanished into thin air. We made our way to the hotel where Mr. DaCosta was waiting for us. This had not been a very pleasant experience.

For a long time I did not have warm feelings toward the Zambian people. But of course I knew that this was not fair. That one man did not represent the rest of the Zambians.

We had dinner and a couple of drinks with Mr. DaCosta. We both thanked him for his assistance and said goodbye because we were not going to see him in the morning. We double-checked our tickets before Mr. DaCosta left just to be sure we knew our itinerary. Understand that neither one of us had been outside our respective countries except as refugees in Botswana. We had never made such a long and complicated journey before. The last thing we wanted to have happen was to find ourselves stranded at some airport with no money and no visas.

Everything checked out well. We needed to leave the hotel at about eight in the morning.

After Mr. DaCosta left we decided to hang around a little longer. This was our first taste of what we called "civilized life" outside a refugee camp. We were like birds that had just been let out of a cage. Besides, this was actually our first experience staying in a big hotel. We both thought it was cool. We shared another drink and began to muse about our ordeal at the immigration office earlier in the day. Both of us had heard stories of people being sent to jail because they did not have transit visas. I was convinced that that man wanted to send us there. I thought that the only reason he made the telephone call to Livingstone was that we protested so vigorously. I also thought that because we seemed to be traveling with a foreigner and a UN diplomat, that appearance might have given him pause to consider our fate more seriously. However, my colleague did not think so. He was convinced that the man was looking for money under the table.

However, since we did not produce anything, he had to find a way to retreat gracefully. The telephone call may very well have been faked. All this seemed to make a lot of sense when you consider how easily our young escort was willing to part with our travel documents. We will never know the truth. The important thing is that we did not spend the night in jail. Instead we slept on comfortable hotel room beds.

The hotel arrangements had been made by the airlines. Back in those days the airlines took care of passengers that had to stay overnight somewhere. We did not have to worry about being late the next morning for our flight because the airline had made arrangements to pick us up. And so, after a delicious breakfast of toast, bacon, and eggs, we left the hotel for our next flight.

We were a little afraid that perhaps our immigration friend might be there again. But fortunately it appeared that this was a different crew. Everything went smoothly. We cleared the immigration gates without a hitch. This was essentially our final hurdle in Africa. Although we were going to make two more stops, we did not have to clear customs again. We were in transit all the way to London.

We boarded a flight to Ndola in Zambia. This was a relatively short flight. But I suppose it was an important stop because there seemed to be quite a few people who came on board there. By now we were feeling like seasoned travelers.

Our stop at Ndola was brief. We were allowed to disembark but had to remain in the transit lounge. Ndola was a copper mining town that had a tremendous impact on the Zambian economy because at the time copper prices were good. Many Southern Rhodesians had moved there to work in the mines and mine-related industries.

I had read about Ndola in our geography lessons. Being there was marvelous, although from the air and from the airport it did not seem to be such a big deal. However, the fact that I had touched down there was interesting.

We boarded our jet again. This time it was bound for Kampala, the capital city of Uganda. All those geography lessons that once seemed dry and useless came in handy. I recalled all the lessons about the Tropic of Capricorn and the equator. This was all a good mental exercise. The reality of it was that I did not have much time to assess all these theories. We were allowed to disembark in Kampala, but once again we could remain only in the transit lounge. The view from the air was incredibly beautiful. I would have loved to spend a couple of days by Lake Victoria. The surrounding landscape from the airport was equally lovely.

Uganda was already an independent country. Pictures of Milton Obote, then the prime minister, were visible in the lounge. It was nice to know that he had the country under control. After all, we were leaving our countries because we wanted that freedom and equality. We wanted a society where every citizen was free to pursue their dreams and aspirations without the color bar. Here the Ugandans had achieved it. Life was tough, but at least they had that freedom to determine their own destiny. This stop was in some respects crucial in my journey. It was the last stop in Africa. As it turned out, it was nine years before

I returned to this airport. My wife and I made a stop here on our honeymoon in June of 1977. But on that bright sunny afternoon of September 26, 1968, I took in the last scenes and sites of the African continent on my outward-bound journey.

We boarded the jet on the last leg of our journey over Africa bound for London, England. I was looking forward to seeing the Sahara Desert. However, I do not recall much of a view. This was another late afternoon flight. We had been traveling all day. The novelty of flying was beginning to wear off. We had a long non-stop flight from Kampala to London. By now the constant hum of the engines gave me both time to reflect upon what this journey meant and moments to dose off and relax. There was plenty of time for both.

I had read in history about the voyages of the explorers and traders that took months and years to complete. Thanks to technology, I had breakfast in Lusaka, in southern Africa, but I was going to spend the night in London, England. Cecil John Rhodes, David Livingston, and Vasco da Gama would have loved that. They spent months at sea to cover the same distance.

I had read and heard about London from the time I first heard about white men and the king and queen. We sang the song "God save the King" (or "Queen," depending upon the year). To us London was synonymous with both. Virtually every textbook that we used was published or printed in London. Our final examinations in high school were set and graded in London. Our university, the University of Rhodesia, was a college of London University. The colonial authority that governed our country and our lives derived its power from London. A trip to this place that controlled so much of my life was indeed something to look forward to with great anticipation.

I asked myself a million questions. What would it be like? Would it be anything like what I had read? I had read about the Thames River, Big Ben, the Underground, the Abbey, St. James, and Bond Street. I had heard about Madame Tussauds wax museum and the changing of the guard. I had listened to speeches from the House of Lords and the

House of Commons. I had read and listened to many announcements from No. 10 Downing Street.

For many years I had waited in vain for an announcement from these halls of power that would set my country of Southern Rhodesia free from colonial rule. I heard of Lord Salisbury, after whom the capital of Southern Rhodesia was named. On this day I would set foot in the land that held so much power over my life. I knew that I would not see much. After all, we were going to land very late at night. I would not even have the chance to take in an aerial view of the city. The lights and skyline of London would have to suffice.

The service in the plane was excellent, I thought. On the other hand, I had very little to compare it to. Dinner was served over the skies of Europe. It was delicious. There wasn't much of a culture shock with meals because I had spent two years at the University of Rhodesia. The meals there were very much in the style of European cooking and service. Granted, there were a few things tailored to meals in flight that were different, such as the individual packages of sugar, salt, pepper, and salad dressing. Once I got the technique of opening all these things down pat, I was alright. I entertained myself by reading what was written on some of these packages. I was curious to know where they were packaged or produced. I was, of course, curious to know if any of the food packages were produced in Southern Rhodesia. This would have been a violation of the economic sanctions against that country. I did not see any.

As night fell, the pilot announced we would soon be landing in the UK. They passed the immigration papers around in the plane. My heart began to pound a little harder. This was the moment I was waiting for. I would finally set foot on the land of my oppressors. It was as if a big secret would finally be revealed. Of course, I knew better. The whole point was that I would finally get to go where the colonialists would prefer that I not go. A dazzling array of lights lit up the land as we approached the airport. I had completed my immigration papers. I could sit and try to see as much as the little airplane windows allowed.

We were approaching Gatwick airport, which I did not know at the time was a good distance from downtown London. We landed safely. I had sucked on my sweets the whole time, so I had no problems with pressure in my ears.

But things were a little more complicated here than they had been at all the previous airports. This was a much bigger place. There were a lot more people going in all directions.

I followed the crowd to the immigration officers. This was always an intimidating point of the journey. Ever since my experience with the Zambian officer who wanted to send us to jail, I approached the officers with some trepidation. I was amazed that these people did not even ask too many questions. The gentleman was actually very pleasant and helpful. He asked me where I had come from and where in the States I was going to. He also wanted to know how long I was planning to stay in London. All the time he was looking through the pages of my passport which was virtually empty. It had only been stamped a few times on this journey. When he was apparently satisfied that I was not planning to immigrate to the UK, he stamped my passport. The stamp clearly stated that I was admitted to the UK for a period not to exceed six months. It further stated that this visa was not valid for employment. A mischievous thought ran through my mind when I saw this. I wondered if such restrictions had been imposed upon Cecil John Rhodes when he came to Zimbabwe.

The gentleman then directed me to a British Airways desk across the way. Since I was only in transit, the airlines took care of my accommodation and transportation needs much the same way as they had done in Lusaka, Zambia. I picked up my luggage and a car assigned to me whisked me to a hotel in London. I do not have the faintest idea where this hotel was. All I know is that it was in a busy area and it was a big hotel.

The airlines made arrangements for me to travel to the airport in the morning. Considering it was rather late at night and we had had dinner on the plane, I did not feel like eating anything. All I wanted was to get a decent night's sleep.

My South African colleague and I last saw each other when we lined up to go through immigration. As I recall, he was still in line when I left. We never saw each other again. It would have been nice to know what became of him. But I guess both of us were so nervous about the journey that the niceties of exchanging addresses were too trivial to entertain. The UK was his final destination.

My hotel room was clean and comfortable. There was music on the radio if I wanted to listen to it. But that was the furthest thing from my mind at this time. I was tired and overwhelmed. I had faith in the airlines that they would not dump me there and forget. They seemed to be very well organized. Even though I was tired, I was anxious to get on with the last leg of my journey. But I had this night to get through.

There was no time to see the halls of power, Parliament, and No. 10 Downing Street. I would not even see the changing of the guard. I certainly would not be invited to have tea at Buckingham Palace. I figured that I would settle for this hotel room. And so I went to sleep.

I got the wake-up call at 7:00 a.m. Otherwise I would have slept through. I must have been tired or the bed was too comfortable. Under normal circumstances I would have been up much earlier than that. I quickly got ready and went down to the restaurant for breakfast, my first meal overseas. It didn't taste any different from the bacon and eggs that I had eaten before. The tea was no different either, which I believe was the Ceylon tea that I was used to drinking back home.

By 8:00 a.m. I had finished my breakfast. To be sure that I was not left behind I went back to my room and got my luggage. I brought it to the lobby where I waited for the car that would take me to the airport. Once again I checked to make sure that everything was in order. I had my passport and ticket, and the visa was stamped inside the passport. As long as I had those items I knew that I would get into the United States. I had come this far, it would have been a shame not to be able to complete my journey.

I knew of situations where it had happened. For some reason some people were not allowed to board the flight to New York. The only explanation was that their visas were not in order.

The car came for me right on time, at 8:30 a.m. I was looking forward to this ride because it was the only time that I would have a chance to see a bit of London from the ground.

The trip to the airport was short but interesting. It took me through the narrow, busy streets of London. Traffic was heavy at that time of day, which I did not mind as long as we would get to the airport on time. The slow traffic gave me an opportunity to see a few things. I was not too impressed by the architecture of the houses. I also thought they were too close to each other. I was definitely struck by the narrow streets. I have been back in London many times since then and still cannot get over how narrow the streets are. I suppose it is the country boy in me that is still looking for the wide open plains and savanna grasslands of the land of my birth.

I was sure glad that somebody knew where they were going. I didn't even know which was east or west. The tall buildings obstructed my view of the sun, and I was totally disoriented. We got to the airport in good time. The place was a beehive of people. It seemed as if people were just rushing in all directions. But actually there was a method to this madness.

Everyone knew their airline. I knew my airline, but I had no idea where to start. The driver was helpful in getting me started. He helped me with the luggage by carrying it into the building. Once inside, he showed me where the ticket counter was. I knew I was in the right place. I joined the line, which looked about a mile long, but went very fast. The ticket clerk asked for my passport and ticket. I had both of them ready.

By now I was familiar with the procedure. I was just nervous in case he found something wrong with my visa. Maybe they spelled some word incorrectly. But when he looked up with a smile on his face I knew I was in. He asked me a few routine questions like what

I was carrying and what my final destination was. He asked me how much money I had and what school I was going to. By then it seemed as if he was just being polite to make me relax a little. He weighed my luggage; of course, it did not weigh much. We got to the seat selection and I asked for a no smoking window seat. Everything went well. He gave me my documents, wished me luck, and told me to go on to the immigration gate. I knew that there was nothing to stop me now.

My luggage was already on its way. This had to be just formality. Well, not quite—the gentleman at the gate was stern. He had that hard military look on his face. He asked me a lot more questions than the previous man. He wanted to know what I had been doing prior to corning to London. He also wanted to know who sponsored me and who was going to support me. By this time I had come to the conclusion that one had to have a certain personality to be an immigration officer. This evoked memories of the Zambian episode where I thought for sure I was going to spend the night in jail.

This time I thought the worst. I thought this man was going to send me back. But thank goodness, he must have found his heart, because he stamped my passport and let me through. I said to myself, *That was a close one.* I was one step closer to getting on my plane. After that there would be one more hurdle to jump: immigration in New York.

By now I was thoroughly confused about the British people. I did not know what to make of them. The last man reminded me of the colonialists that I had left behind. They didn't want to have anything to do with black Africans. On the other hand, the man at the ticket counter and the driver had been perfect gentlemen. Whatever the case may be, it did not matter anymore. I was now on my way out of the UK and on to the USA.

I found a seat at the gate. I could not wait to get on the plane. In the meantime I occupied myself with the scene on the ground as seen through the large glass windows. There were funny-looking cars and trucks buzzing up and down, ducking under the wings of airplanes. There were small tractor trailers pulling chains of luggage carts. It was a scene reminiscent of ants building an anthill. Everybody was busy and they seemed to know where to put every piece of luggage or whatever they were carrying.

Considering the large number of airlines, the different destinations and the large number of pieces of luggage, they did very well. I believe most people made it to their destinations with their luggage intact. At that point in time I had no clue where my luggage was. I could only hope that the system worked as well for me as it seemed to work for others.

At midmorning the first call for boarding our flight came through. A large number of people stood up. It seemed as if there were thousands of people, but of course there were only a couple of hundred people going on that flight. That was the moment I had been waiting for. I knew that once on board there was no stopping me. Even Ian Smith's long arm of the law could not reach over and grab me now. I walked onto that plane, found my window seat, and settled down for a long flight. This was still not the final flight.

I was going to change planes in New York to continue my journey to Minneapolis. It was midmorning London time. The itinerary said we would arrive in New York at about 1:30 p.m. At first I thought this meant the flight was only three and a half hours until I realized that there is a five-hour time difference between New York and London so that in actuality the flight was about eight and a half hours long.

It was a comfortable flight. The service was decent. Looking down shortly after takeoff, I was fascinated by the aerial view of London. Then as we traveled farther out, I saw the outline of roads, highways, and the land and presumed that by now we were over Ireland, if my geography served me right. And then, there was nothing but the blue waters of the Atlantic for an eternity.

After a while this gets to be boring. I have made the trip across the Atlantic Ocean many times since then. I prefer the journey going toward Europe because it's usually during the night. I have no problem sleeping all the way. That way I arrive in Europe in the morning well rested.

This time I was not that bored because of anticipation. I did not know whether something unexpected might suddenly appear in the ocean. So I kept looking out. I tried to read, but it was not too interesting. I dosed off every now and then. But for the most part I just sat there and thought about everything under the sun. Most of my thoughts were, of course, about what I was about to do and where I was going to be.

I was going to Minnesota. I had no idea what to expect. Even all my geography lessons could not have prepared me for it. I was going to study. However, I had been told that the American system of education was different from our British type and that the system of education was very "broad." I did not understand what that meant.

Did that mean the examinations covered a wide range of topics? Or did that mean I had to take many different subjects? Every now and then I thought about what I might have been doing at that time had I been at the refugee camp or back in Zimbabwe.

I kept myself occupied for some time playing around with the different time zones. I had learned quite a bit about this in my geography studies. But I had no idea that I would one day actually be using that knowledge. We always thought that geography was an important subject in the British system of education for political reasons. We had often heard the expression "the sun never sets in the British Empire." Since there were British citizens in colonies all over the world, it was important for them to know where their relatives were around the globe.

Because of the different time zones it was important to know when to call. This time zone thing has since become very important and real to me. There is a six- or seven-hour time difference between New York and Zimbabwe. So if I don't want to wake up my relatives in the middle of the night, it is important to know what time it is there before I make a phone call. I guess I can now say the sun never sets in my world.

This was a pretty full flight. I tried to estimate how many people might be on the plane. Since I had all the time in the world, I started by counting the number of seats in my row. I was going to walk around and count the number of rows in the plane. Then I was going to sit down and crunch the numbers. When I got up and looked carefully I realized that not all rows were the same. I also realized that there were just too many people to be walking around counting seats and rows. I figured that if I really wanted to know the number it would be easier and more accurate to just ask the airline staff. I never got around to doing that.

Lunch was served over the blue waters of the Atlantic Ocean. I don't recall what was on the menu, but do remember that I was still fascinated by the packaging of all the bits and pieces. The sugar was not in a sugar bowl as I was used to seeing it on the ground. The flatware was in a plastic bag with a paper napkin wrapped around them. The word *napkin* threw me off a bit at first. That word was what I was used to calling baby diapers. *Surely they don't mean that baby diapers are used at a dinner table*, I thought. Well, that was just one of the first lessons that I had to learn. There would be many other words to learn later on—either to pronounce differently or learn a different meaning.

I had an interesting experience related to this difference in meaning when I went back home for a visit a few years ago. I went to a supermarket and ordered five cases of soda for a party. The man brought me five cases of club soda instead of "cold drinks." And I had been taught to pronounce *Z* as *zed*, but in the States they say *zee*. It took me a couple of years to get used to the way Americans speak.

Fortunately I did not have too many questions to ask on the plane. The airline staff was pretty good. I suppose they were used to dealing with international passengers who spoke different languages and had different accents. Now after all the years of listening to Americans, the British actually sound truly foreign and even hard to understand sometimes.

Finally, I looked out the window and saw land. Although the pieces of land that I saw were still surrounded by water, it seemed clear to me that the United States of America could not be very far. My heart began to pump a little harder in anticipation of my arrival on US soil. I was finally almost at the end of my journey.

The hum of the engines continued, with no sign of the plane slowing down. This plane did not have the passenger readout that I have seen on South African Airways which tells you the distance traveled, speed, altitude, and path toward final destination. The best I could do was to guess that we would probably be landing in a couple of hours. I could live with that. The airline staff cleared the tables. Passengers started to move up and down the aisles. The scenery through the windows became much more interesting because I could see what looked like towns and villages interspersed by trees and roads. I am not sure where we were exactly, but believe we were somewhere over the east coast of Canada and New England.

As we came down inland I was fascinated by the yellow, gold, and brown colors of the treetops. It was fall foliage as I had never seen before.

When the staff began to distribute immigration papers, I knew that we were almost there. A certain degree of anxiety came upon me. I would be going back to those immigration officers again. I had no idea what to expect. I only hoped that they would not be like that man who wanted to send us to jail in Lusaka. I really had no reason to be afraid because my documents were all in order. After all, they had survived the scrutiny of immigration and customs officers some seven times on this journey. I filled out my papers like a pro. I answered all the questions as clearly and fully as I could. I had written down the address and telephone number of where I was ultimately going, which was my sister's house. A voice from the cockpit came over the speakers and announced that we would be landing soon. The captain described the weather conditions at JFK Airport as sunny and pleasant. All this was music to my ears. I just wanted to get a glimpse of the Big Apple.

I had heard and read a lot about New York City. I wanted to see those famous skyscrapers that so many had described and marveled about. My seatbelt was fastened already when the stewardess called upon everyone to return to their seats and fasten their seatbelts. I could not tell where the city began because I was so taken by the mass of buildings. It seemed as if there were no streets between them. This was just an awesome view.

The plane touched down to the cheers of many passengers. I got the impression that there were many first-time visitors to New York City who were just as excited as I was. The airline staff welcomed us to New York's JFK Airport and asked everyone to remain seated until the plane had come to a complete stop and the seatbelt sign was turned off. With all the excitement bubbling to the surface I do not believe too many people paid attention to that last request. As soon as the plane came to a halt people jumped up and scrambled for the overhead bins to get their luggage. I didn't have much to scramble for.

I was also at a disadvantage because I had the window seat. If I stood up I would have to bend over until I could gain access to the aisle. The window seat is great for viewing the scenery, but bad if you want to get out in a hurry. I was in no hurry because I had a few hours to kill before my flight to Minnesota.

After what seemed like an eternity I got out of the plane and followed the crowd to those dreaded immigration and customs officers. I had to clear customs here because I had to change terminals in order to catch my next flight. There was a mob of people. It was hard to imagine the weight of the airplane with so many people on board suspended in the air for eight hours. But this was precisely why I had always been fascinated by science—all branches of science. Physics, math, and chemistry had combined their efforts to overcome the power of gravity.

I breezed through immigration without a hitch. My documents were clear and in order. I was coming into the country as a student. I had the proper F1 visa. The address for my final destination was valid, as was my passport. Everything was just perfect. The officer had no trouble reaching for that stamp, which read: US Immigration New York

No. 515; admitted September 27, 1968. With that, he handed me my passport and waved me through. I was finally on US soil.

Even though I had not cleared customs and technically I had not reached my final destination, there were no more legal hurdles for me to jump. There was no reason for me to fear customs because I was not carrying any contraband. The only problem that I might have had with immigration or customs was that I had no money on me. I do not believe I even had a dollar. Remember that at the refugee camp we were getting only two rand per week for pocket money. We barely made it to the end of two days with that money.

In the end, I had no problem going through customs. This had been one of the easiest immigration and customs formalities that I had been through so far.

I emerged through the sliding doors to a huge crowd of people waiting for their friends and relatives. Of course, no one was there to meet me. This was in stark contrast to where my journey began, Francistown airport. I was one of probably four or five people who had boarded the plane in Francistown. The number of people accompanying passengers or waiting for someone to arrive was probably fewer than twenty. Here I was with hundreds of people zipping about like bees at the entrance of a beehive, trying to find my way to the Northwest Airlines terminal. If this was the end of the rainbow, I did not like it too much. It was too hectic for me. For the first time I felt like I was really on my own in the jungle.

All through this long journey I had been in transit. The airlines had taken care of me. Everything had pretty much been there in one place. Here I had to find transportation to get to the other airline. It was an interesting experience. I found out that I could take a free bus ride around the airport and just get off when it stopped at or near my airline terminal. I found my way to the correct terminal and the correct check-in counter. There was no problem. Now I had a few hours to wait. I did not have anybody's telephone number except my sister's. Otherwise I would have liked to take a trip to Manhattan to see the skyscrapers. I settled for a view through the glass windows of the airport. There was plenty of action to keep me awake.

I was only about two and a half hours away from my final destination. However, it felt like I was still days away. I could not wait to meet the people that had done so much for me. My life would be changed forever because of them. As I paced up and down the corridors and waiting rooms of the airport, I was thinking of how I could repay these people for everything that they had done for me. I had no money at all, so a financial means to express my thanks was out of the question. I figured that working hard and doing well in my studies was probably the best way to thank Grace, Ronald, Louise, Leon, and Ginny for believing in me. They gave me the opportunity of a lifetime. They enabled me to climb up to the top of the mountain. I shall forever be indebted to them. They are my heroes.

Finally, very late in the afternoon I boarded a Northwest airplane bound for the Twin Cities, Minneapolis and St. Paul. I did not know then but I was to spend five years of my life in the Twin Cities. By now I was quite comfortable with flying. After all, I was boarding the plane for the sixth time in three days.

I had already logged almost twenty hours of flying time and more than ten thousand miles. I was exhausted and suffering from a bad case of jet lag. However, the excitement of being where I was and knowing where I was going was enough to keep me upbeat.

Not much happened on this flight. Everybody was just intent on getting where they were going. A member of the airline staff offered me a newspaper to read. I don't think I read much of it. I looked at the paper, but my mind was already in Minnesota. I had no idea what this place looked like. I had just come from the semi-desert area of Botswana. A large number of people there were pastoral farmers. They concentrated on cattle ranching. Those that lived and worked in the cities did so in various small service industries such as hotels, restaurants, and department stores. The diamond mines that have since been discovered did not exist. I had seen a little bit of the hectic pace of life in New York City. But I knew that Minnesota was a big farming state.

The question then was whether life was going to be closer to that of Botswana or the topsy-turvy Big Apple. I could never have imagined then that I would eventually settle down in New York City. But such is life. In fact, now I live just ten or fifteen minutes away from JFK, where I first set foot on US soil.

The plane touched down in Minneapolis just as the last rays of the sun disappeared in the distant horizon. There was a chill in the air as we passed through open spaces along the arrivals corridor. I was bubbling with excitement. My eyes were all over the place, partly to take in the scenery, but more importantly, to see my family. I did not know where they would be. So I looked everywhere and at every face like a cameraman panning with his video camcorder. The joy in my heart when I saw my sister was beyond description. It was not just the joy of seeing her after so many years, but the gratitude that I felt for what she had done for me. One could have seen tears in my eyes. She was there with her husband, Ronald, and my pen pal and sponsor Louise.

Louise had seen pictures of me. But I had not seen any of hers. So this was the first time that I was seeing her. She was just as beautiful as she was kind. I had not met my brother-in-law Ronald either. However, it was as if we had known each other for years. He was warm, charming, and very pleasant to be with. They'd had a long day because they knew I was coming on that day, but I had not confirmed what flight I was going to be on. They had called everywhere to find out which flight I was going to be on.

Among their concerns was whether I would be allowed into the country, considering where I was coming from. In those days, the kidnapping of people involved in politics was not unusual in Southern Africa. But as the expression goes, all's well that ends well. I was finally in the Twin Cities—tired, but safe and sound. I was ready to turn to a new page in my life. I was so determined and so focused that I could not wait to start school. But of course, the proper arrangements had to be made.

# Chapter 10

# Minnesota

* * * * * *

T he air was crisp and biting when I arrived in Minnesota. It was typical fall weather in that part of the world. But for me, it was colder than winters in southern Africa. Late May, June, July, and early August are the winter months in Zimbabwe and Botswana. I arrived in the Twin Cities on September 27, 1968, just in time for the brutal winter weather typical of the Upper Midwest. I took it all in stride. Two winters in one year was not going to kill me. My mind was focused on something else.

I had prepared myself mentally for the changes I would face. However, on that first day my jet-lagged body was overwhelmed by the emotions evoked by coming face-to-face with the people who had done so much for me.

I arrived with my luggage intact. There wasn't much to speak of. The drive from Minneapolis International Airport to St. Anthony Park in St. Paul seemed to take but a minute. There, in my sister and brother-in-law's one-bedroom apartment on Como Avenue, I was to spend my first night in the United States. I was tired.

I had been traveling for three days. My hosts had prepared a delicious meal and invited a few friends over for dinner. I had a lot to talk about, and there was a lot that they wanted to know. However, because of the lateness of the hour we had to put some of the stories on ice. There would be plenty of days ahead for us to sit around and shoot the breeze.

Among the many people that I got to know was a young student from Botswana by the name of Ernest Serema, who became my roommate. He was a student at the University of Minnesota. It was an incredible coincidence that our first names were the same, our last names were very similar, and I had just come from his homeland. My pen pal Louise found us a basement apartment in the house of a University of Minnesota professor. Serema and I shared this place for about a year. It was convenient in many respects. It was in a quiet part of town called St. Anthony Park. We had a separate entrance to the house, and more importantly, it was very close to my sister's place. Since we had no cooking facilities, we ended up eating practically all our meals at my sister's home.

Our bachelor pad, as we called it, was actually no more than a bedroom. We had bunk beds right across from the laundry room. There was barely enough room to move around. Somehow we created enough space for two chairs that we used for studying.

The ground rules didn't allow for any parties. We had no room for them anywhere. We didn't have a refrigerator because there was no room for one. The ground rules also did not allow alcoholic beverages. Since my sister and brother-in-law did not drink alcohol either, we were stuck. We found a fellow African student from Tanzania who lived close by. He had a refrigerator where we could keep our drinks for those occasions when we felt like it.

Once I got over the jet lag I was able to meet all the people that had come together to make it possible for me to come to the USA. I met Leon Knight, a college professor and an accomplished poet with an incredible knowledge of Africa. Born and raised in the Midwest, he had taught in Zimbabwe. He fell in love with the African people, their culture, history, and politics. Leon understood the predicament that I was in when I wrote letters from Zimbabwe asking for help since he had been there.

I met his wife Ginny, an accomplished artist and poet. I did not know this at the time, but I have since admired many of her drawings and paintings. I have also read many of her writings. Ginny, a lovely, warm person, has been a mother to many African students in need. Over the years I have maintained contact with Leon and Ginny. I have continued to draw inspiration from their work. They have enabled many students to come from Zimbabwe to study in the US. I have enjoyed their writings and Ginny's art work. They are two giants with broad shoulders. I am grateful that they have allowed me to stand on those shoulders so that I could see far.

In my language we have an expression that says "A true friend or relative is always willing even to share the leg of a locust." To the best of my knowledge the leg of a locust has hardly any meat on it. But this was the situation with my sister and brother-in-law. They were both students at the University of Minnesota. They were barely able to sustain their own livelihood, but they were willing to share the "leg of locust" with me.

One of the first things that I needed to do was to get some warm clothes to face the frigid temperatures of the Midwest. I had never seen snow in my life. I had never experienced anything colder than the low thirties. When they talked about temperatures below zero I really could not imagine how I would survive. When they talked about snow, I tried to imagine mounds of frost which we get in the early mornings in June in Zimbabwe. During the winter months in Zimbabwe, the frost generally kills any unprotected vegetables and plants. Here they seemed to be telling me that the ground would be covered with snow for months. It did not take much persuasion for me to realize that I needed warm winter clothes.

Given our cash situation, buying new clothes was out of the question. So we headed to north Minneapolis where there was a Goodwill store. It was our favorite store for a number of years. With less than fifty dollars, we were able to get a whole winter wardrobe that would last me for a few years.

I was still trying to get my bearings when we went to the Goodwill store in north Minneapolis. One thing that was clear in my mind was what a humbling experience this was. My brother-in-law, Ronald, had been a successful businessman back home. He had done well for himself in Zimbabwe by any measure. His only crime was to love his country enough to want to fight for it. Once he got involved in the struggle for the liberation of Zimbabwe, he became a target for the colonial regime. His story has never been told, but it brings tears to my eyes.

He left the country with nothing but the clothes on his back. On that day in north Minneapolis he was buying second-hand clothes, not to give away, but to wear. I learned that he did this because he, too, had his eyes on a much higher prize. He had decided that no matter how hard the colonial regime tried to silence him and break his resolve to free the Zimbabwean people, he would not let them do it. They had taken his businesses and destroyed them. He was going to get an education and use different tactics to prosecute the struggle for what was his birthright.

Ronald was a grown man and doing his undergraduate work at thirty-seven years of age. The energy and discipline with which he approached his studies was incredible. It is no wonder that in five years he was able to complete his bachelor's degree, his master's degree, *and* his PhD in agricultural economics and education at the University of Minnesota. Very few people have ever managed to duplicate what he did. He set the tone for me. I knew that if I kept my focus like Ronald did, I would reach the top of the mountain.

After graduating from the University of Minnesota, Dr. Ronald Sibanda and my sister went on to work in Zambia where he had lived as a refugee before going to the US. He helped the Zambian farmers improve their farming techniques in order to be economically successful. From there he went to teach agriculture to young students and communal farmers in Botswana. He earned his wings as an educator. Even in retirement his services are still in demand throughout Botswana. He is a man who believes in leadership by example. So they bought a farm in which they demonstrated that good agricultural techniques can lead to successful agricultural economics. They established businesses in which they sold the products from the farm. They sold fruits and vegetables. They sold meat in a butcher shop. They established a restaurant and bakery which utilized many of the products from the farm. Over the years I have learned a lot from Dr. Sibanda. I will forever be grateful for the things he taught me and for his unwavering support.

There is no doubt in my mind that when my father died in 1970, he felt comfortable leaving me in the hands of my sister, Grace. She has been my mentor. When I was young and searching for direction, she stood tall at Mpilo Hospital and showed me that I could find a career in health care. In 1968 I was disillusioned and desperate. She heard my cry from the refugee camp in Francistown. Once again she rose to the occasion.

She mobilized perfect strangers for me and put together a coalition that enabled me to come to the States. Grace has been the unsung heroine of our family. With her quiet intellect, rock steady determination, and insightful mind, she was never afraid to lead. She was the first Simela to become a registered nurse. She sailed through nursing school with high honors. To my knowledge she was the first Simela woman to own and drive a car in a male-dominated society. She was one of the first Simelas to venture across the border of Zimbabwe in pursuit of fertile ground to advance her career. In so doing she opened doors for many of us.

In her career she has nursed many wounds and broken bones. She has comforted thousands of broken hearts and families. As a midwife, she has helped thousands of women to safely bring their infants into this world. There are nurses all across southern Africa, and indeed around the world, who owe their success to her role as a nurse educator. To me she is still my big sister to whom I can go when it hurts. I owe my career to her. I shall forever be indebted to her.

Oftentimes when I reflect upon my life and the struggle to the top of the mountain, I attribute many of the obstacles I encountered to the white racism that existed in Southern Rhodesia. However, it is ironic that among the people who helped me to get to the USA, a great deal of the credit goes to a white woman by the name of Louise Platt.

Introduced to me as a pen pal, young Louise was as warm, beautiful, and generous in person as she had been in her letters. In 1968, when everything seemed to go dark around me, her letters always turned the lights on. When I was at the refugee camp in Botswana, she heard my desperate cry for help and responded generously with a rescue plan. Louise not only helped me to get to the States, but she made sure that I had a place to stay and helped me with funds to start school.

When I met her parents, I knew that there is truth to the expression "the apple does not fall far from the tree." They were the most beautiful, warm, and pleasant people I had ever met. I enjoyed many hearty meals at their house. I have pleasant memories of Louise's attempts at teaching me how to skate on the frozen lakes of Minneapolis. I also recall with joy the warm sunny days canoeing around the lake by her house. It has been people like Louise and her parents who made this world a beautiful place to live in. I am very grateful for the role they played in my struggle to the top of the mountain.

There was hardly any time for adjustment because the school year had already started. I was too late for the fall semester. We had to make some changes in where I would go to school. Hamline University was much closer to where I lived. It was also on a much better calendar system for my purposes. They were on a quarter system rather than semesters. This meant that I would wait only about two months to start school during their second quarter. I went to the school to sort out the admission process.

They gave me an English examination which I thought was pretty easy. I met two people who would later play a major role in my education and career decisions. One was Dr. Wesley St. John, the foreign student advisor. He was amiable, gray-haired, and well-traveled. He was also a professor of political science.

Dr. St. John made foreign students feel at home at Hamline University. He was attentive to every little problem that we had, from the petty personal and financial type to academics. During the four years that I spent at Hamline, I saw only two foreign students leave the university because their problems could not be resolved.

And I met Dr. Olaf Runquist, the chairman of the chemistry department, who also taught organic chemistry. I owe my career to Dr. Runquist. He was my academic advisor. Of course, I majored in chemistry and biology. Upon looking at the statistics on admissions to medical schools across the country I did not think I had a chance.

I looked at all the things that were stacked against me. I was a foreigner, black, and my grades were not the best. Dr. Runquist looked at all the positive things about me. He said I was determined, bright, mature, and my grades were not as bad as I had thought. He urged me to apply to medical school.

When I brought up the issue of money, he went out of his way to make contacts with various people and organizations who could help. In the summer of 1972, I even prepared Plan B in the event that I did not get into medical school. I applied to Akron University for a master's degree in microbiology and was accepted.

Dr. Runquist would not give up. Finally, in November 1972, only seven days before the deadline for submission of application forms for medical school, I sent mine in.

It was almost exactly a month later that I received a letter and another form from Albert Einstein College in the Bronx. I was asked to complete the form and return it as soon as possible. Needless to say, I was very excited that someone even looked at my application. Dr. Runquist was even more encouraging because he saw this as a good sign. I filled the forms out immediately and sent them back.

A few weeks went by before I received a letter inviting me to come for an interview. This time the excitement was almost impossible to contain. I could see the crack in the door. It was not yet big enough for me to put my foot in, but the surge of the adrenaline was there. I told myself that if I could just put my foot in, I would give it everything I had to succeed.

I was working at Hennepin General Hospital at the time. I requested a couple of days off to go to New York. My coworkers were very supportive. In fact, I recall that one of the nurses, Suzzana, gave me a medical dictionary as a present.

I took Greyhound from St. Paul bound for New York. It was a long journey, about twenty-seven hours. I could not have done it any other way because I did not have the money to fly. My interview went well.

A few weeks later, in February of 1973, I received a letter of acceptance into medical school. This was the climax of what had been a very interesting experience of over four years in Minnesota. Two things had dominated my life from the time I arrived in Minnesota until this point—work and school.

A few days after I had arrived in the Twin Cities, I got my college admissions process cleared. I registered to start school at Hamline University in early December 1968. I had already nailed down my accommodations. I was going to live off campus. The rent was fifty dollars a month.

The next thing was to find a job so that I could at least partially support myself. I got a job at Target. This was all new to me. It had nothing to do with anything that I had learned in school or experienced. The store had a system where a customer's goods were put on a conveyer belt after the customer had paid for them. There was some kind of identification card placed on them. The customer would then bring their vehicle around to a pick-up point. My job was to load their goods into the car. For this I was paid $1.40 an hour, or $11.20 a day.

I had to take two buses to get to work. In the end, the cost of transportation and the travel time did not make this a suitable job for me. So I looked for another job.

Fortunately, it didn't take long to find one. This time I needed only one bus to get there. The pay was a little better. I worked as a stock boy at G. C. Murphy stores in the Midway Shopping Center. By now I had been in the country about two months.

A lot of things were beginning to make sense. I understood people when they spoke, even when they used slang or abbreviations. Nothing annoyed me more than the use of abbreviations that one could not find in any dictionary. People tended to use these abbreviations assuming that since I lived in the Twin Cities, I must understand or know what they were talking about.

My job at G. C. Murphy was a valuable experience. This was a department store with a wide range of items. It also had a garden shop where they sold plants and flowers in the spring and summer. In the winter there were snowmobiles and other winter sports related items. Working in the storerooms exposed me to all these items. This way I got to know what Americans like in terms of clothing, jewelry, foods, sports, and other outdoor activities. I interacted with a lot of young and middle-aged people who worked in the store in various capacities.

A lot of women worked in the basement sorting and labeling goods before they were put upstairs on the floors. They talked about their day-to-day lives, their families, and what their children were doing. It gave me an opportunity to know what a cross section of Middle America did when they were not working.

The people I met at G. C. Murphy represented a wide spectrum in terms of income levels, race, and education. Many were housewives who worked only a few hours a week. Some were college students working part-time like me. There were others for whom it was a second job. This was something that I had not seen much of in Zimbabwe. I don't know whether it was because of the scarcity of jobs in Zimbabwe, but I had not known many people who held two jobs.

Of course, many people, like my father, worked at a steady job and did some farming as well. This could be considered a second job. There were seasonal workers as well. They worked during Christmas or in the summer. These were people just looking to make some money for gifts or vacation expenses. They came from all sorts of backgrounds. They were headed in every direction in terms of future plans or careers. The shopping center was called Midway and was situated between St. Paul and Minneapolis.

The diversity of employees and the customers during the Christmas season seemed to represent the crossroads of America. It was an interesting time to work the floors. I stayed at G. C. Murphy for more than half of my college years at Hamline. I got to know the manager very well. I believe he got to know and trust me, too. I doubled as a cashier in the garden shop during the summer. I always worked afternoon and evening hours because I went to school during the day.

In the summer of 1969 I decided that since I was not going to go to summer school I would look for a second job. I found work at the Minnesota State Fairgrounds. Minnesota has a big annual state fair in September. It is the biggest fair that I have ever seen. I worked with groups of people who helped to prepare for the fair. There were a lot of things to be done, ranging from cutting grass, planting and cultivating flowers, to setting up the stands. They had music tents where popular musicians performed live.

I remember the year Johnny Cash came. Everybody was talking about him. I suppose because I was not a music enthusiast I did not know much about him. I was told that about a million people were expected to come to the fair because of him.

Our team leader was a schoolteacher during the rest of the year. In the summer he supplemented his income by working at the fair. He was a jolly fellow who enjoyed being outdoors. They had a spectacular fireworks display at the end of each evening. To me, this was worth the price of admission.

While I enjoyed working at G. C. Murphy and at the fairgrounds, the pay was low. One summer I decided to look for something different. I found a job in a coke factory. This was not the coke you drink, but a place where they burn coal and turn it into coke used for heating.

Soft coal is heated to extremely high temperatures until some of its gases have been removed. The remaining solid, carbonaceous material is used as fuel. This was a dirty, hard job. However, it paid well at $3.60

an hour. Most of the time I worked in the area where we unloaded coal from railroad cars.

We brought each car in one at a time. The car was positioned over a giant hole in the ground, known as the hopper. Using huge sledgehammers, we pounded the doors until they opened. The coal would fall through into the hopper. A big black cloud of coal dust filled the air each time. I often wondered what the health effects would be from having been exposed to so much coal dust.

From there the coal was carried on conveyer belts to the ovens. After it was heated, it was drenched with large quantities of water. The cool, dry coal was then sorted and graded according to predetermined standards, then loaded into boxcars bound for destinations across the country. The next railroad car would be brought down and the whole process would be started again.

There were a few things to learn. It didn't take a genius to do this job, but it required certain acquired skills. The process of bringing the boxcars down to the hopper involved releasing the brake just enough to allow the wheels to roll. Sometimes one had to initiate the movement of the wheels by some kind of push on the wheel itself. Once the car was in motion, it was critical to control its speed. Otherwise, the car would go past the hopper. Pushing back on boxcar loaded with coal was not easy.

On the other hand, it took a lot of force on the brake wheel to stop a fully loaded car once it was in motion. I had an experience where I was almost seriously injured while trying to stop one of these cars. The brake is applied by turning a wheel located at the rear upper left corner of the boxcar. Since this is too high up to reach from the ground, one has to stand on a step at the rear of the car. One day I tried to stop a car, but it was going too fast. The more I turned the wheel, the faster it went. It went past the hopper and banged into the car ahead of it. The impact of this collision knocked me right off my feet. Fortunately, I hung on to the braking wheel and escaped falling onto the railroad tracks.

I was scared half to death. The man who was working with me was an old man who could not even run to help me apply the brake. This man had worked the same job for over thirty years. I wish I could have seen his chest X-ray.

There was no easy job in this factory except perhaps one. They had this old giant crane which was used for loading coke into box cars. The thing was ancient and humongous. There was only one man, Mr. Herman, who knew how to operate it. It had what looked like a million levers. You had to know which levers to pull or release at what time in order for the crane to open, close, lift, or drop. I tried this machine and failed miserably. But Mr. Herman was up there all day in his overalls. He made it look very easy.

The company recognized that the work in this factory was physically hard. They provided a number of water fountains since the men were sweating profusely all day long. We were even provided with salt tablets. The job was so dirty that we were allowed half an hour at the end of the day to shower before going home.

The only good thing about the job was the pay, which I thought was very good. I saved enough money over the summer to buy my very first car. I bought a used Plymouth Belvedere for two hundred dollars. I loved that car—and why not? I worked hard enough for it.

The end of summer meant it was time to go back to school. I always scheduled my classes in such a way that I had time to work. Most of my classes were in the morning. For the first two years this worked well. It allowed me to work at G. C. Murphy in the afternoons and evenings. But Murphy pay was not enough to cover all my expenses. At some point I joined a cleaning company that offered jobs at night. The supervisor took us to various locations such as banks, car dealerships, and other businesses. They would drop one or two people at each site depending upon the amount of work involved. They would lock us in and go to another site.

Each person was allotted a certain amount of time to do whatever they had to do. The supervisor would return to check up on our work and to lock up the place. I learned how to use the tools of the cleaning trade. The one tool that I had a hard time mastering was the buffing machine. Whenever I tried to use it, it would fly in all directions. I was always afraid that I would break something, especially when we did furniture stores and other places where there was merchandise on the floor. In time I learned how to control the machine like a pro.

My partner was an amiable gentleman by the name of Pat Purisi. He taught me a lot of tricks about the cleaning business. He taught me how to wax and buff the floors and make them so shiny that you could almost see yourself. He had been doing this for a long time. He eventually decided to start his own business doing the same thing.

Since the hours were so convenient, I didn't hesitate to join him as an employee. This worked out very well because he understood my situation. He gave me the flexibility I needed for school.

By the time I got to my fourth year in college I had an apartment at 721 Snelling Avenue, which I shared with my brother Oscar. He was by then a student at St. Thomas College in St. Paul. My sister, her husband, and I sponsored him. We paid for his ticket to come to Minnesota and helped him with his initial educational expenses. After that he worked this way until he got a PhD from Kent University. I had a lot of work at school, especially because of the laboratory experiments that I was conducting. I did some research work both in biology and chemistry. My days and evenings were not so free anymore. I definitely needed something to do at night. I found a job in a bar on University Avenue in St. Paul. This bar was open until about 1:00 a.m.

I would come in at that time to clean the place using the skills that I had learned from Pat Purisi. Once I was done with all the cleaning, I would restock all the coolers with beer and other types of drinks. I was left in there by myself all night. I could not go out because I didn't have the keys. So I essentially served as the cleaner, stock boy, and security guard.

My boss, Mr. Mertens, was the owner. He came in early, about 8:00 a.m. I would then go home and to school. It was rough, but it paid the bills and took me a step closer to realizing my dream.

One summer I tried selling encyclopedias. I worked for a company that took in a whole bunch of salespeople like me, mostly students. They would drive us to designated areas and give each of us several blocks of houses to work. They took us to a remote area in the south of Minnesota. People hardly opened their doors when I rang the doorbell. I'm not sure what role skin color played in all this, but I didn't sell a single set of encyclopedias. When I got back to St. Paul I decided that selling encyclopedias was not for me.

Fortunately, it was not very hard to find work. The very next day I went to an employment agency and got a job with a company that was moving furniture for Levitts. We were carrying furniture from a warehouse to a store. The supervisor was so nasty to the workers that I decided at the end of the day that I was not going to do this to myself. I remember saying that I thought slavery had been abolished many years ago. To me, working for this man seemed to represent a form of slavery.

So I moved on. I always joke about the fact that of all the crazy jobs that I took, the one area that I never ventured into was the kitchen. It's true: I never worked in any place that involved cooking, serving food, or washing dishes. I don't know if it was that I didn't like cooking or simply a coincidence. I don't even remember looking for a job in any place like that. But my brother worked at the Red Barn fast-food chain.

Minnesota is a major farm state. We got to know people whose families were still living on farms and some who owned farms. This was helpful because we saved a lot of money on food by buying directly from the farmers. A group of us used to get together and buy a whole cow. The farmer would slaughter it, cut it up, and package it according to our instructions. Then we would put the meat in a deep freezer. This way we could go for a long time without having to go to the supermarket. Naturally, it meant that we had to cook our meals at home. Otherwise the temptation was always to hit the pizza store or the hamburger joint down the road.

We also bought apples and made apple pies. We had a lot of fun doing this as a group. There were other fruits and vegetables that we bought depending upon the season. The whole objective was to save money, and we did.

Life in Minnesota was not all work and school. Incredible as it may seem, there was a sizable number of Zimbabwean students in the Twin Cities, as well as students from many other parts of Africa. We got to know each other even though we attended different colleges. Many students attended the University of Minnesota.

A substantial number of students went to other colleges such as Hamline, McCallister, and St. Thomas. Because all these colleges are in the Twin Cities, we had a lot in common. On weekends we had get-together lunches and dinners. There were parties for those so inclined. People in general were very friendly. Students mixed and mingled with the local residents easily.

One of the things that I enjoyed was camping. Whenever I got the opportunity to go, I went with friends to places like Duluth, Lake Superior, and beyond. On one of the last occasions, we followed the Gun Trail all the way up to Sue St. Marie. There we set up our tents in the middle of nowhere. During the day we went canoeing on one of the cleanest lakes I have ever seen. It was refreshing to go around in a canoe. The water was so clean that you could look at the bottom of the lake and see nothing but fish.

One night I was terrified when the bears came around to the trees right next to our tents. I had been told that if you bang pots and pans the bears will run away. So we made the loudest noise with our pots and pans. Sure enough, the bears disappeared. We had a lot of fun. I enjoyed the fresh air and being outdoors.

There was another activity that I enjoyed during my stay in Minnesota. I do not recall exactly when I first met the remarkable lady named Mrs. Gregason. She was part of an organization called the Christian Fellowship. They had a beautiful place, a mansion in the suburb of Eden Prairie. This place was used as a retreat.

Mrs. Gregason invited us on many occasions to spend weekends there. They had a beautiful swimming pool and other sports equipment that we were free to use. We could just sit and read, sleep, or shoot the breeze with other people. The building was a magnificent mansion set on the slopes of a quiet valley. In the winter there was a breathtaking view of the snow-covered trees and grass up and down the valley. You didn't have to go outside to enjoy the view. There was a glass wall on the valley side of the house where you could sit and dream.

It was a perfect place to see the seasons change. You could almost see the snow melting away and the trees and flowers coming to life in the spring. The birds and deer had no fear as they enjoyed the open space in the valley. Slowly, right before your eyes, you could see the leaves turning from green to the yellow and gold fall colors. This was a nature lover's paradise.

For us it was also a place to come for some peace of mind. We prayed and shared meals with people from all over the world and all walks of life.

I had started school in the middle of the school year, in December 1968, and so in December 1972, I completed all my courses on time. But the university held graduation ceremonies only once a year, in May.

I didn't want to start anything else in the middle of the year. Besides, I was still in the process of applying to medical school. I decided to look for work. My advisor helped me to get a job at 3M Company. I would have been doing research work in either the field of pesticides or something dealing with polymers. Unfortunately, I could not take the job because I needed to be bonded. Since I was only on a student visa, they could not hire me. I was disappointed, but it didn't take long for me to get another job.

I was employed by the Minnesota Medical Association, which ran a dialysis unit in south Minneapolis. I worked as a technician. This was the best thing that I could have done. It brought me as close to the medical field as I had ever been. Although my job was to make and dismantle the dialysis machines, known as the *Keils*, I had the opportunity to speak to patients. Most of the patients had regular schedules for their dialysis. Some spent the night there and went to work during the day. I got to know and understand how important kidneys are. This was the first time that I saw firsthand how an illness can change the lives of so many people.

It was also the first opportunity that I had to see how technology was applied to save lives and improve patients' quality of life. I moved from the Chronic Unit in south Minneapolis to the Acute Care Unit at Hennepin General Hospital. There I saw very sick patients on dialysis and even candidates for a kidney transplant.

All the time, I thought to myself, one day I would be on the other side as the doctor. Only a few months later, I started medical school at Albert Einstein College of Medicine in New York City.

# Chapter 11

# Hamline University

⊛    ⊛    ⊛    ⊛    ⊛    ⊛

Before coming to the States, the only university campus I had known was the University College of Rhodesia. It was a fairly large and beautiful campus. This was a place that was supposed to set a higher standard of living than what the average Zimbabwean was accustomed to. People were generally well dressed in suits and ties, even when they were just going to class. We were expected to wear graduation gowns to the dining halls. The service in the dining rooms was equally impeccable.

It is therefore not surprising that I was a bit shocked when I arrived at Hamline University. The students were wearing just about anything that they could lay their hands on. There was no dress code. The relationship between students and faculty was extremely casual.

Hamline University, a private institution located in St. Paul, is the oldest college in Minnesota. It had been kept small by choice, as far as I know. This allowed it to provide quality education almost on an individual basis. The classes were generally small. The professors and instructors were always available to their students. There was a family atmosphere throughout the campus.

There were only about fifteen hundred students, many of whom, like me, lived off campus. There were dormitories available for a few students, lived in primarily by students from out of state or who lived too far to commute.

For new students, this was probably the best school. It was hard to get lost. Everything was right there. Classrooms were on either side of the administrative offices. The student center was right nearby. If you couldn't find something, it would take less than five minutes to find someone who knew where to go. People were very friendly. Even a perfect stranger would take time to show you where to go. That is why even so many years later I have fond memories of this great institution.

One of the ironies about Hamline University was its racial mix. I had attended the University of Rhodesia where race relations were a big issue. The ratio of black to white students was about 1 to 5. Here in the whole school there were fewer than ten black students, a ratio of about 1 to 150. The big difference was that there was peace and harmony in the school.

Each student was an individual. Each student was evaluated on the basis of merit and not the color of his or her skin. When I started, most of the black students were foreigners; therefore, we had a lot in common. We formed a foreign students association of which I was once president. However, since we also had African-Americans in the student body, we also had a black students union. Over the four years that I was at Hamline, the black student population grew to almost one hundred.

We had a fairly diverse foreign student body. There were students from Africa (Zimbabwe, Kenya, Nigeria, Tanzania and Uganda), Iran, Iraq, India, Israeli, Switzerland, St. Kitts (in the Caribbean), China, Japan, Chile, Korea, and Panama. Many other countries were represented over the years. Diverse as this student body was, the very fact that we were not from the United States brought us together in a way that I have not seen since.

We had weekend parties together. The most important link was our foreign student advisor, Dr. Wesley St. John, and his wife. They invited us to their home many times. It was like our home away from home. We learned a lot about each other's countries and cultures. Sometimes we brought traditional food from our countries and shared it. In this way we had a taste of what various countries ate, even though we had never been there.

During the time that I was a student I participated in a Model United Nations Program. This reinforced my interest in international activities and the diversity of cultures. Many students participated in this program. We represented several countries within the United Nations. We studied the way in which the countries we represented participated at the United Nations. We checked their voting record and tried to understand the forces behind any trend in their voting patterns. Sometimes the clues were in the political structure and division of power. Sometimes there were enormous economic forces to contend with. Whatever it was, we tried to know as much about the country and its people as possible.

We traveled to St. Louis, Missouri, where the Model United Nations sessions were held. My group represented Zambia. Here we met students from other colleges who represented other countries. We conducted sessions in a manner that was as close to the actual United Nations as we could. We had the General Assembly and the various committees as they are constituted at the United Nations. The topics that we debated had been selected in advance. Our job was to debate these issues and come up with resolutions or recommendations. Our opinions were supposed to mirror what the actual countries would have discussed. We had some spirited debates and a lot of fun. It was a great learning experience.

I had the opportunity to put the knowledge that I gained at the model United Nations to use some years later. I became chairman of our liberation movement, ZAPU (Zimbabwe African People's Union) in the late seventies. Our organization had observer status at the real UN, and so I spent a great deal of time there listening to many international issues being debated.

We listened and shared in some real discussions when the issues related to the struggle for Zimbabwe's independence came up. It was interesting to see how the various issues wind their way through the halls of power around the globe. These had become real-time debates— real issues about real people. Decisions made here affected the lives of millions of people.

During the time that we were attending the model United Nations sessions in St. Louis, we tried to make our experience as real as possible. Each night we went to a restaurant that served meals from a different country and culture. One day we went to a Mexican restaurant, on other days to French, Italian, and Chinese restaurants, and so on. Unfortunately, there was no Zambian restaurant.

We all had heard the expression "The way to a man's heart is through his stomach." At the end of these sessions we agreed that the best way to appreciate a people's culture was to know and understand their diet.

When I went to Hamline University my mind was so focused on my studies that everything else around me was almost invisible. I could not stand being distracted even for a few hours. I felt like that would cause me to fail in my mission. I was going to the top of the mountain, even if it meant that I had to forego all the fun and games enjoyed by college students.

My major field of study was going to be science. That is what I had done at the University of Rhodesia. You have to understand that in the British system of education the sciences are almost completely separate from the arts. I couldn't believe that I was expected to take physical education courses for credit. As far as I was concerned, that was a waste of time. I was shocked when I found out that I had no choice. I would not be able to graduate without physical education courses. So I signed up for swimming and golf.

I did well in swimming because I enjoyed it even in high school. But then I was doing it for recreation and competition. I had never touched a golf club until I took the class. I knew next to nothing about it. I'm not sure I learned much during the course. I know I made it around the links.

This early exposure to what I had considered a waste of time had a profound impact on my view of American education. My colleagues in science were not like wooden robots who had no appreciation for the environment in which they lived. They loved and understood the American popular sports like football, baseball, and golf. Outside the science lab, they lived like everyone else because they had learned to cultivate a broader view of life. As I went on to take courses in the liberal arts, I understood that the intention was to give me more options in life. I was not married to science. I could be a scientist and still have an understanding and appreciation for other subjects. After all, I could end up being a politician someday. It would not hurt to have an understanding of international affairs, or to have a basic knowledge of economics.

The news on the radio, television, or the print media is not limited to scientific articles or to arts and entertainment. By taking various courses I was able to follow discussions and analyses of a wider variety of subjects. I admired the depth that was emphasized by our system of education in Zimbabwe. But I felt that it was too restrictive. Students were forced to make choices about their future long before they'd had a chance to see what was out there for them. Thus, I went on a spree and took courses in all kinds of subjects such as English, literature, history, political science, economics, and even a foreign language. I took German, which I thought was very difficult.

One of the courses that I enjoyed very much was comparative religion. This was one of those courses for which the small class size at Hamline University was really well suited. We had the opportunity to carry out lively discussions in which everyone participated.

While most of the discussions centered on Christianity, Judaism, and Catholicism, there was a much wider range of subjects and religions discussed. One of my classmates was from Israel. He was a highly vocal student, raised within Judaism, so for him the aspects of the discussions relating to Judaism were real-life experiences. There were many Catholics and non-Catholic students in the class. This made for some really interesting debates. It just seemed as if there was something for everyone. That is what made this course so rewarding. The teacher was dynamite. She was able to lead the discussions, ask questions, and make comments without being judgmental.

After going on this wild fishing expedition, sampling all kinds of subjects, I came back to the core of my studies—science. I didn't like physics much. Fortunately, I didn't have to take too many courses in it. I was, and still am, fascinated by many theories in physics. I have great respect for such great physicists as Isaac Newton.

My dislike for the subject probably started when I was doing my A-levels at Fletcher High. I had a teacher there that I did not like. He just turned me off completely. I thought he was prejudiced and not a nice person at all. He was not a good teacher either.

When I came to Hamline University, even a veteran Professor like Dr. Kent Bracewell could not spark my interest in physics. Dr. Bracewell graduated from college in 1927. He had been teaching at Hamline University since 1931. He taught me in 1969, which means that he had been teaching the same subject at the same university for almost four decades.

He had seen a lot of changes in science and technology. He had learned and used an array of teaching methods and had seen all kinds of students pass through his classes. Dr. Bracewell knew every trick in the book for handling college students no matter how interested or disinterested they may have been in his subject. I guess he bombed out on me. Physics was just not my bag.

The mathematics department was small but taught by seasoned professors. Dr. Flemming was not just a veteran professor, but a first class gentleman. I had always loved mathematics so didn't need anyone to convince me to take it. I always thought that mathematics is fundamental to science. Perhaps subconsciously I thought that if I was to be a true scientist I had to learn mathematics. Whatever the reasoning was, I just seemed to enjoy the subject. Unfortunately, I didn't know quite what I could do with it besides teaching.

It's unfortunate that I did all this before the age of computers. I was in my third or fourth year of college when Wang computers were introduced to the department of mathematics. The computers fascinated me. But there was so much work to do before a person could use one, such as making the program cards.

I'm absolutely amazed at how far and how quickly technology has grown, even in my time. I enjoy tinkering with electronic gadgets. Perhaps if I had started out in today's technological age, I might have found myself immersed in the world of computers and electronic toys.

However, that was obviously not to be my destiny. I took many courses in mathematics, but I didn't make it my major.

I don't know if it was the farm boy in me, but I was attracted to the life science of biology. In my childhood, our way of life revolved around living things. Boys were either herding cattle, sheep, and goats, or cultivating crops in the fields. Girls were either in the fields or cooking for the family. Studying biology was a logical thing for me to do. I had learned to identify various plants, trees, and grass by the way they looked. Sometimes we identified them by the smell of their leaves. We knew which plants were edible and which ones were poisonous. We also knew which ones grew in various types of environments. When we learned about ecology in biology, it all made sense to me. It was something that I had observed since childhood.

Unfortunately, the types of plants that I knew in Africa were different from the ones we learned about in Minnesota. However, the fundamental principles were the same.

I wanted to graduate with honors in biology. To do this I had to do a research project. My advisor in this project was Dr. Ellis Wyeth. He was excellent. He gave me good advice. But he also let me do my thing as much as possible.

My project dealt with bacteria. I found bacteria called *Serratia marcescens* which is sensitive to changes in the environment in which it grows. The bacteria changed colors or did not grow, depending upon the temperature of the environment. Based upon these and other observations, I concluded that it was possible to cure diseases caused by bacteria by altering the pH of the environment. For example, if one had a urinary tract infection caused by bacteria sensitive to low pH, one could limit the growth of the bacteria by acidifying the urinary tract. I also concluded that perhaps the reason for the rise in body temperature when one is ill is a natural way by which the body limits the growth of bacteria.

Our grandparents believed and many people today still believe that the best way to deal with a febrile illness is to sweat it out. They cover themselves with blankets. There may be some merit to this practice. My research showed that when you raise the temperature as our grandparents did by covering themselves with blankets, bacteria did not grow and multiply. By so doing, the body defended itself against bacterial infections. I successfully defended my paper and graduated with honors in biology.

All the science classes were held in the science building. The ground floor was used by the mathematics and physics departments. The second floor housed the biology department and the third floor was chemistry. I spent a great deal of time in that building. In addition to taking various courses, I had my research projects to deal with. I did them during my spare time, which was limited.

In chemistry I analyzed milkweed. I learned that in some parts of the world, such as Mexico, milkweed is used for medicinal purposes. It is used to cure warts. I set out to discover what the active ingredient in milkweed is. It was a pretty interesting project.

My favorite professor, Dr. Runquist, was my adviser. I gathered bags of milkweed and set up an extraction process. From those bags of raw weeds, I recovered very small quantities of material, which I analyzed. I used a variety of methods, including spectrophotometry and diffusion. The only thing was, the work required Job's patience.

I had to pay attention to a lot of detail. I came up with a chemical structure of what I thought was the active ingredient in milkweed. This was a tremendous educational challenge. I never got a chance to test my extract on real warts. Who knows—I might have discovered a cure for those pesky warts that never seem to go away.

In my senior year I had to do a lot of juggling with my time. I carried a full load in school because I wanted to graduate as soon as possible. I also had a job outside school. I was working in the science department as a lab assistant in the chemistry and biology classes. This was a lot of fun.

In the biology labs we had a number of field trips. We went to places like the breweries to see how they produce beer. We learned about the fermentation process. We also went to the Gillette Company in St. Paul. Here we learned about the preservation of products such as shaving cream and other cosmetics. It was interesting to see the application of theories that we had learned in biology class. I don't know if my students enjoyed it as much as I did. But everybody seemed to be listening attentively.

The students knew that they would probably be tested on the materials that they learned on the field trips. I, on the other hand, went there just to keep order. I was in charge. The students were no problem. I was responsible for driving the station wagon that we used on those field trips.

At the end of the semester the students were given forms to evaluate our performance. They all gave me excellent marks as an assistant and thought I was a good teacher, but they weren't so sure about my driving. We had joked about this throughout the semester. I assured them that they were in good hands. This was one of the good things about Hamline University. The small size of the classes allowed for an unusual interaction between students and teachers. Even as a lab assistant I was always only a few feet away from every student. We joked and laughed as we learned. When we piled into that station wagon, we were like family.

When I started out at Hamline University I lived in St. Anthony Park. It was the first time in my life that I had seen snow. I didn't know how to deal with it. The winter was too cold for me; having to struggle through piles of snow and ice made it worse. In fact, I fell on ice one day and sustained an injury to my hip that has plagued me ever since. Most of the time, I took the bus to school.

Because of the closeness of the people in the school, I found help. The director of the alumni office, Mr. Lowell Weber, lived in my neighborhood. He often saw me waiting for the bus and would offer me a ride. He was kind enough to tell me that I could come to his house and catch a ride with him every day. I thought that was very nice of him, and I appreciated this kindness very much.

Whenever I had morning classes, which was almost every day, I went over to Mr. Weber's house. There were many days when the windshield of his car was covered with ice. This was new to me. He would just scrape a small window on the windshield on the driver's side so that he could see where he was going. The rest of the snow and ice would melt on its own.

To this day I am amazed and still wonder how people survived winters in Minnesota before houses and cars were heated. I have visited places like Plymouth Village in Massachusetts and the Quiet Valley Farm in Pennsylvania. Both of these places depict the lifestyles of early settlers. They managed to stay warm by burning wood and covering themselves with warm woolen clothes. At the Quiet Valley Farm they also show how children were swaddled and tucked under the parents' bed.

But these people had to be outside some of the time. Winters in Minnesota are long and very harsh. When I arrived in Minnesota it was early fall. I had just been through winter in southern Africa. I had bought flannel shirts for winter there. I barely used a coat during winter months. In Minnesota I could not put on enough clothes. I had long johns, warm winter pants and shirts, heavy sweaters, a heavy winter coat, a hat which covered my ears, a scarf, and gloves. I walked like a mummy. No wonder Mr. Lowell felt sorry for me and gave me a ride every day.

When I decided to look for an apartment, I wanted something that would be as close to school as possible. I found a place right across the street from the University on Snelling Avenue. In the winter I could run and get to school in less than five minutes. Of course, when there was ice, I had a problem.

That apartment was so convenient that I could run home in between classes and never miss anything. It was also a quiet place that gave me the privacy and peace of mind I felt I needed to study. I shared the apartment with my brother. He was not a problem because he also had his own mountain to climb. We both seemed to be incredibly determined to achieve our goals. We went to different schools and had different circles of friends. But when we came home, we both had one thing in common—a desire to succeed in our studies. There was no loud music to disturb the other person. There were no friends in the wee hours of the night to disturb the other's sleep. My brother eventually earned a PhD from Kent State University.

I had tried to live in the dormitory for one semester. From my perspective it was a disaster. There were a number of reasons that explained why I was so unhappy. For one thing, I was a little older than most of the students in the dorm, and so a lot of the college student craziness that went on was simply not something that I appreciated. The music was not my type of music; yet it was always so loud that I couldn't help but hear it. There was so much noise in the whole place that even if I closed my door I could still hear it. It seemed to me as if the students spent more time socializing than studying.

This was contrary to my resolve to achieve a career within ten years. The environment didn't support my core beliefs; so I left after only one semester. I moved to a place close enough that I was able to do the same things that I did when I lived in the dorm. I had moved into the dorm for the convenience of location. For example, when I lived in St. Anthony Park, it was hard to take a bus home after school in the afternoon and then return in the evening for some function. Sometimes I had to go to work after school and then return to the library to do some research for my projects. Without a car, some of that traveling back and forth was almost impossible. But living across the street from campus made life a whole lot easier.

My father died just as I started my second year at Hamline University. This was a big blow to me. He was my father, my hero, and my role model. He had worked hard all his life to give us whatever we had. It had been my hope that I would one day to see him again when we could sit down and relax together. I had never seen him do anything but work.

My parents never knew what a vacation was. They never did any traveling other than something related to work or the death of a family member. For a short while, his death crushed my spirit. I felt like there was really not much to work hard for. He was gone and I was not even able to bury him. But then I quickly regained my composure and refocused my mind.

In a letter that he had written to me about one month before he died I found reason to go on. He expressed his happiness about the fact that his children were united and helping each other. He said that even if he died he would be happy knowing that we would always help each other. And so I felt that my goal should not change, because that is what my father died thinking I would do. Besides, my mother was there. Whatever I wanted to do, I wanted to do it for both of them.

By then almost half of our family was in St. Paul. The weekends and evenings were no longer as lonely. We could call each other from work, home, or wherever. It was not like trying to call Zimbabwe, where one had to book a call and wait a couple of hours for it to go through. Calls to my hometown were routed via London, then Harare (which was called Salisbury), and finally to Bulawayo. But even then one had to call somebody at work because no one had a telephone at home. After all that trouble, the cost of each call was prohibitive.

My sister's house in St. Paul was always a good place for a home-cooked meal. We took advantage of that whenever time allowed.

There were a substantial number of Zimbabwean students in the Twin Cities. We used to gather together at someone's house or some location every now and then. This helped to take away some of the loneliness. No matter how good life may be wherever we are, many of us still miss home. There is something strong about where one's roots are. Perhaps it is the anchoring characteristics of roots that we don't yet fully understand. Even after all these years, I still have a strong yearning for my homeland.

I must have buried some deep roots at Hamline University as well. I have fond memories of the place. But I feel like I missed out on a lot of the life of the college because I was so focused on my studies. I also missed out on a lot of the functions because I had to work many hours to pay my tuition. Hamline University had a strong physical education department. I participated only to get the two physical education requirements out of the way. I wish I'd had time to play tennis or baseball, or even to learn something about football. This word was confusing to me. Back home when we talked about football we meant soccer. So I never got into American football at all.

Some of my friends in the science department played on the football team. But since I didn't even understand it, I didn't know what all the hoopla was about "touchdown." I know now because my son swears by it.

There were some very active and good teams in various sports at Hamline University. Given the kinds of winters that Minnesota is famous for, it made sense that the college had an excellent hockey team. In the winter there was ice everywhere. The lakes were frozen. The roads were frozen. And even the Mississippi river was frozen. You could skate virtually anywhere. In fact, you could probably get to where you were going faster on skates than if you tried to walk. Unfortunately for me, this is one of the things that I tried to learn but failed miserably in.

Two friends took me to a lake in Minneapolis. I donned my skates without any problem. Then it was time to stand up. I could not imagine how in the world I was expected to stand up on a sharp knife. So they held me and dragged me to the center of the lake. Each time I tried to skate on my own, I fell down. At the end of the afternoon I gave up. I just could not overcome that fear of falling. Perhaps if I had done this when I was younger, I would have done well. Otherwise, I really enjoyed watching people skate. I think it's absolutely fascinating, one of the most graceful sports—especially when accompanied by music. Perhaps when I retire and have all the time in the world, I will learn how to skate.

There were many colleges around the Twin Cities and throughout the state and great competition among the students of various schools. Hamline University was right there in the thick of it. Even though I did not compete or go to these games, I was always impressed by the results. According to the 1971 Hamline University yearbook, the swim team was excellent. They placed second in Minnesota Intercollegiate Athletic Conference (MIAC) competition. They broke thirteen varsity records. There was a lot of talent and a lot of competition in the school.

The tennis team tied for second place in MIAC competition. When I look back I cannot believe that something as big as the MIAC could go by without my noticing it. But the truth is that's exactly what happened. I was so involved in my own quest for the top of the mountain that nothing could distract my attention.

Now I look back and wonder if I could have been more involved in college activities. I wonder if it would have changed anything in my life. I wonder if I might have taken a different path than the one I took. The most important question that I have asked myself is whether I could have spared any time for those activities. The answers have been consistent. In order for me to do what I had to do, I needed total concentration. If I had tried to do other things, I would not have been able to do any of them well.

It takes hard work and effort to perfect a sport. I could never have had the time to practice and still work the hours that I worked. On the other hand, I fully recognize that I missed out on a great learning experience. I could have become an excellent tennis player under coach Lowell Weber, the man who used to give me a ride to school. I'm sure he would have given me a few tips on our ride in from St. Anthony Park.

So I didn't participate in sports, but I read the college newspaper, *The Oracle,* an excellent source of information about life on and about campus. *The Oracle* was great and fair. It included letters from students and faculty who praised, criticized, or questioned it. It was awarded an All American rating by the Associated Collegiate Press for two consecutive semesters in 1970 while I was at Hamline University. The newspaper was not just well written but informative. It reported on the achievements of the Pipers' sports teams. That was how I followed the activities of various sports teams.

It also reported on things like the development projects on campus—the construction of new student residences and the destruction of Goheen Hall to prepare for construction of the new library. It even delved into the controversy over the *4 – 1 – 4* system. This was the calendar year which gave students and faculty about one month in January and February either to continue taking courses on campus or go off campus and do whatever they could organize. I did not go off campus because I couldn't afford to. But I liked the idea. If I could have, I would certainly have seized the opportunity to attend some special course, seminar, do research, or take a class abroad.

Then there was *The Liner,* which summed it all up. This beautiful yearbook captured the stories, life, and activities of the year and the people involved in them. I love the pictures because they bring out the youth in all of us. The pictures sum up stories that could not be told in a thousand words. I think this should be a major part of every college. One can look at *The Liner* for 1971 and see such faces as the Honorable Shirley Chisholm, the first black woman to serve in Congress, addressing the students. In the same pages one can see Mr. Charles Evers, mayor of Fayette, Mississippi, also addressing the student body. There were events sponsored by PRIDE (Promote Racial Identity, Dignity, and Equality). Black students made their presence on campus known. They brought issues of race that confronted the country to the attention of everyone. Pictures show members of Give-A-Damn displaying their smile and pride. This was an organization that tried to help each of us to become a little more sensitive in a confused and often cold world. Members of the organization worked with children who had difficulty adjusting to school socially or academically.

There were organizations of every stripe. All abbreviations in Webster's dictionary were used to name the organizations. There were organizations with Greek names whose meaning I do not know to this day. There were Alpha Tau Omega, Tau Kappa Epsilon, Theta Chi, Pi Beta Gamma, Alpha Rho Delta, and so on. There were persons who were already environmentally conscious. They belonged to the Environmental Concern Organization. They sponsored Earth Week in the spring. The International Relations Club sponsored the Model United Nations in which I participated. The Foreign Students Association, captured beautifully in pictures of the 1970 *Liner,* sponsored an International Travel Fair. I was president of this organization once. There was even a Republican Club. Two of its members held offices in the state organization, the College Republicans of Minnesota. They sponsored speakers and panel discussions on a broad array of topics. Every student in the school could find an organization that they could identify with. That was the beauty of the Hamline University Community.

Commencement ceremonies are generally routine affairs, though not to the graduates. It is also a wonderful day for the parents of the graduates, who reap the rewards and fruits of their labor. This is the day when they see that helpless infant they brought from the hospital finally bloom. All those sleepless nights and all those diaper changes are finally rewarded. For the graduates that day marks the end and the beginning. It is the end of usually four years of hard work and sometimes sleepless nights. When that paper is due the next day and you are on page one at midnight, it means a lot of coffee for many hours. Sometimes the examination presents a big challenge when the subject matter is not easy to understand. Whatever the case may be, the graduation ceremonies mean that everything has been done. All the i's have been dotted and the t's crossed.

It also means this is the beginning of responsibility. Mom and Dad have been there for all your needs. On that day it usually means that they can relax and watch this toddler take a few unsteady steps. They will usually be there to catch the toddler when he or she falls. For the student it is also the beginning of responsibility to society. Now these graduates go out to work, pay taxes, and much more.

The commencement ceremonies of 1970 were anything but routine. The country was still at war with Vietnam, and the chants of protests against the war were getting louder. The calls for the end of the war were increasing. The civil rights movement was very strong. Hippies were calling for peace. The Black Panthers were in jail. Calls for their release were as loud as ever.

The late Hubert Humphrey was a senator from Minnesota for many years. He served as the thirty-eighth vice president of the United States under Lyndon B. Johnson. In 1968 he was the Democratic Party's nominee for president. He was invited to speak at the graduation ceremony at Hamline University in 1970. Protesters interrupted Mr. Humphrey's speech with loud chants about the war in Vietnam and freedom for the Panthers. He eventually abandoned his prepared remarks and addressed the protesters directly. He told them that if they thought politics was so dirty they should get their own soap and bucket and clean it. Then he continued to talk to the graduates about social responsibility. On that day he was given an honorary degree by Dr. Richard P. Bailey, the college president.

On that day he was given an honorary degree by Dr. Richard P. Bailey.

Dr. Richard P. Bailey, the president, was Hamline University's greatest asset. He was involved in every aspect of the college's activities. When he was not being presidential in his office, you could see his face all over campus. He was out greeting freshmen one minute and talking to their parents the next. He was seen talking to faculty and administrative staff. He was there as MC at a talent show and at the coronation of the homecoming queen. Hamline University was his responsibility and he wrote about it as such. He wrote beautiful, inspiring letters to the Hamline community. I always enjoyed reading them and kept many. When the climb to the top of the mountain was rough, I often turned to them for inspiration and motivation.

Hamline University was home to me for four years. It gave me a chance to mold my career and get a firm grip on the slippery slopes of the mountain. Hamline University is where I learned all about America, the American system of education, and the American way of life. It was Hamline University that opened the doors of possibility for me. Before I was accepted to medical school, I was accepted at Akron University for a master's degree in microbiology. Who knows—I might have become the microbiologist to discover a cure or vaccine for AIDS.

Hamline University opened the door for me, gave me the compass, and showed me the way to the top of the mountain. I will always have fond memories of that citadel of higher learning and the many people there who helped me through those dark, cold days of my life.

Chapter 12

# Albert Einstein College of Medicine

＊　＊　＊　＊　＊　＊

When I took that long bus ride from St. Paul, Minnesota, to New York, I could barely see the peak of the mountain that I was climbing. It was three thousand miles away and four years up a steep incline. My determination was stronger than ever. My eyes were so fixated on that peak that the long journey was not a concern to me. I had all my meager belongings with me. More importantly, I had my mind, body, and soul together with me.

I had resigned from my job as a kidney dialysis technician at Hennepin General Hospital. Even though I enjoyed working in the dialysis unit, I had my eyes set on a higher goal. I carried with me the best wishes of all my coworkers. Some hoped I would return to Minneapolis as a nephrologist someday. Others wished me the best in whatever I chose to do down the line.

I had visited my academic advisor at Hamline University the day before I left. I thanked him for all his encouragement and confidence in me. I promised him that I would not disappoint him. He wished me well and gave me three hundred dollars that he had raised on my behalf. Dr. Runquist knew my predicament. He knew the fire and determination in me, but he also knew that I had absolutely no resources to put toward this big project. He was not going to let that stand in my way, and he convinced me that I should not let it stop me from setting my goals as high as I wanted to go. I will forever be grateful to him for believing in me. He was a great teacher. But more importantly, he is a good-hearted man.

The bus started off from the streets of St. Paul, a city that I had called home for almost five years. There was a sadness in me as we pulled away. I was leaving behind once again what had become familiar surroundings. I had made friends with many people here. My life had become predictable and comfortable. The Greyhound bus was taking me to a whole new life in a city known for its complexity and intrigue. I took my seat in the bus and told myself—ready or not, New York City, here I come.

The wheels rolled and the engine roared as we made our way out toward Wisconsin. It was a beautiful June day. There would be no camping in the Great Lakes for me this year. There would be no more reading by the Mississippi River and no more canoeing on the lakes of Minneapolis. As we passed Stillwater and crossed the river into Wisconsin, the Twin Cities faded away like the sunset on the distant horizon.

I had been on this route once before when I went to New York for my interview. I had an idea of what lay ahead. There would be cities and hamlets interspersed by long stretches of highway and farmlands. There would be many stops at truck stops and rest places for people to stretch their legs and get something to eat. We had some thirty hours of travel time ahead of us.

Even though the seats were comfortable and the bus was equipped with toilet facilities, I could sit for only so long. The scenery was absolutely marvelous. The plush green trees and manicured lawns and gardens with colorful flowers were everywhere. Cows and horses interrupted the long stretches of highway. The stream of cars and trucks in both directions was a constant reminder of how mobile this society had become.

One by one the bus swallowed the states like Pacman. Many passengers shared intimate conversations while others enjoyed music from their Walkmans. Some dozed off from time to time and others seemed fascinated by the scenery. This reminded me of my childhood days, when we had our first experience as passengers in a car. We were fascinated by what seemed to be moving trees. I was kind of lost in my own world. I decided to see and enjoy the beauty of the country as much as I could. It was not often that I got to travel across the United States by road. This was my chance, and I was going to make the most of it.

I was not used to sitting down for long periods of time, and so those truck stops were a great relief. They gave us an opportunity to stretch our legs. People streamed out of buses to use toilet facilities and get a bite to eat. But sometimes it was just fascinating to stand and see the activity moving in and out of the truck stops.

As night fell, we had covered a considerable distance. The journey was beginning to take its toll. Many more people were dozing off than those still engaged in conversation. But our able driver kept on spinning the wheels. There was an almost eerie calm when we cruised through lonely farm areas where there was not much traffic and there were no lights. It was at times like this when the real meaning of this journey began to sink in. This was a step up that mountain—a major step, because now I could see the peak of the mountain, although it was still a long way off. I had at least identified the exact spot where I would go to get the letters MD; that place was called Albert Einstein College of Medicine.

As I sat there in the bus my mind was going through steps that I would have to take in order to achieve my goal. The bottom line was to work hard every single day. There would be no partying. There would be no drinking. I would make use of every resource at my disposal. This was a once-in-a-lifetime opportunity. And I was not going to let it go to waste.

The driver pulled into a bus terminal somewhere. I believe it was in Chicago. Some people woke up and got out for a stretch; many chose to stay and enjoy their zees. I figured that I would get out and step on the ground. At least I could say that I have been to Chicago. The man that had been sitting next to me also got out. It turned out that this was his final destination. Our driver also got out with all his equipment. This was also his final destination for the night. A new driver was going to take us from here.

While I was out milling around the station, I struck up a conversation with a pretty young lady who seemed to be anxious to get on the bus. Her name was Tracy. She had just graduated from the University of Chicago and had decided to take some time off to travel and see the world. She was going to do it the cheapest and most exciting way. She wanted to experience every adventure and every challenge that one could come across on such travels.

Tracy was well read. It seemed she had read every adventure story ever written, from the journeys of Christopher Columbus to the adventures of Marco Polo and Vasco da Gama. She knew about the culture, politics, and social life of many parts of the world. Tracy was planning to start her journey by bus and travel around the United States before venturing beyond the borders of her own land. I thought that was a great idea.

Tracy had a smile and personality that matched her beauty. She also had the intelligence and eloquence to crown it all. I envied her agenda. But I had my own struggles to face. Tracy got off the bus in Philadelphia and I never saw or heard from her again.

The sun was up when we pulled out of Philadelphia. My conversation with Tracy had made the hours go by quickly. There was a lot more traffic now that we were in a big city and everybody was up. This slowed our pace. The scenery was much more interesting. There was a lot to see and a lot more activity. There were many more towns and villages along the road. The passengers in the bus were up and a lot louder than before. I tried to figure out what this meant, but I couldn't come to any conclusion. I didn't know if the people were just excited about getting to their final destination, or were not as laid back as the people in the Midwest.

After living on the East Coast for all these years I've come to the conclusion that people out here tend to be a little more excitable than those in the Midwest. We were definitely approaching the Big Apple.

It was not long before the unmistakable skyline of New York City appeared in the distance. The tops of the World Trade Center towers appeared to pierce the clouds. There was a serenity and calm that seemed to fall over the rest of the skyscrapers. Plumes of smoke twisted in the wind above the buildings and then melted into the clouds above. The lulling hum of the bus engine had turned into jerky roars of the stop-and-go traffic. It seemed to me that getting into New York City at rush hour was not a very good idea. The last few miles of this long trip were agonizingly slow. I learned then that traffic jams were a part of life in the big city. Fortunately, I was not driving, because I was not ready for the frustration caused by traffic. Finally we pulled into the Forty-Second Street bus terminal.

There was no one there to meet me. But, I didn't expect anyone either. I thought I would find my way to the college. However, I had not done my homework on this one. I had no idea how far Albert Einstein College of Medicine in the Bronx was from Forty-Second Street. I figured that I could catch a taxi. That was an eye-opener.

I took a yellow cab from the bus terminal in rush hour. The driver took me through some twists and turns that almost made me dizzy. By the time we got to the college we had asked the whole town for directions. The meter was reading over fifty dollars. My funds were limited to start with. Now I was tired and depressed over this huge expense I had not anticipated. But what could I do? I paid the man and he went his way.

Albert Einstein College of Medicine is located in the northeast part of the Bronx. Since there are no other courses or studies besides medicine, the campus is small. The driver had dropped me off at the dormitory. The staff and students there were very helpful. They offered to keep my luggage while I went to the admissions office to complete the registration process. Everything went well.

I was assigned to room 440 in the dormitory. This room, hardly six feet by ten feet, was to be my home for four years. If I stood in the middle and stretched my arms I could touch the walls. There was a small bed and a small desk and chair by the only window. There were no cooking facilities in the building. In fact there was not much besides these small rooms. There were a few offices located down the hallway on my floor. These were larger rooms because they were at the end of the hallway. We also had some exercise equipment down in the basement. This became one of my favorite places. We needed a key from the receptionist–telephone operator to get into the gym. I developed such a regular routine that when the receptionist saw me at about 10:00 p.m., she just handed me the key.

The dormitory was conveniently located near the classrooms, the library, and the Albert Einstein College Hospital cafeteria, for those that could afford the cost of the food. Many of us, especially the minority students, did not have the funds to buy meals there. The college had made arrangements with Van Etten Hospital down the street for us to purchase tickets for our meals there. We paid twenty cents for breakfast, thirty cents for lunch, and forty cents for dinner. The meals kept us alive. We also got a little exercise walking back and forth between Van Etten and our dormitory. This was a humble existence. But I don't believe that any of us were looking for luxury at the time. I venture to say that perhaps the less distraction the better it was. Study was the keyword.

I had been to college for a few years. I had done a lot of reading, studying, and practical work in the field of science. However, this seemed to be a whole new game. Perhaps the myth around it being "medical school" played a big role. The studies were focused on the human body. That, too, probably brought issues of responsibility to bear. This was no longer a paper or a science project that could go wrong and nothing would happen. People's lives were at stake. You had to learn it right and do it right the first time.

The first year was especially intense. We studied basic science, including anatomy, biochemistry, pharmacology, and physiology. Most of us had been introduced to these courses before. But the depth and detail that was covered in a such a short period of time left my head spinning. There was little time to fully digest this amount of material. I found myself studying all the time. But after a while I would reach a point of diminishing returns. That's when I went to the gym.

There was a lot of interesting and challenging material to learn. One of hardest subjects was anatomy, ordinarily a pretty dull subject. In high school, students dissected frogs and other small animals. Basically, you learn that this is a heart, lung, or kidney, and so on. But when you have a human body in front of you, it changes the whole game. The first day that you have to take that knife and cut into human flesh changes your state of mind, not just for the day but forever. I once listened to a discussion in which somebody said that medical school is not about learning but about transforming. I believe that a lot of that transformation begins on that first day in the anatomy class.

For a few days after the first encounter with a cadaver, many medical students become vegetarians. It's hard to go from that lab to the cafeteria and eat meat without thinking of the human body and its parts that you have been slicing. However, like everything else, one gets used to it.

One of the most interesting things about anatomy for me was the way in which I always compared it to the body parts of a cow or goat. You will recall that when I grew up, we slaughtered cows and goats for our consumption. My parents went on to operate a butchery in which cows were slaughtered every day. So when I studied anatomy I drew on a lot of images from those past experiences. I wished that I had known then that I would have to study anatomy in the future. Anatomy might have been my favorite subject.

When I was growing up we knew where to stab a cow in order to kill it. A spear to the side of a cow would go directly to the heart. Some people used a knife to the back of the neck. There was a large measure of knowledge of the gross anatomy.

At Albert Einstein, neuroanatomy was a big thing. I began to understand that when you put a knife to the back of the neck you actually sever the spinal cord. This in turn essentially paralyzes everything. Ultimately breathing stops. When I was young I saw experts in my father's butchery business killing cows by putting a knife in the back of the animal's neck. I did not understand why the animals died. When I took the neuroanatomy course I learned that they were actually severing the spinal cord.

As we wove this tapestry of medicine and the human body, all the subjects that we took began to make sense. It would be hard to understand the physiology unless one understood the anatomy, the parts of the body and how they relate to each other. Once we understood normal physiology, then we could understand when things go wrong. When the normally almost invisible thyroid gland becomes large and forms a visible lump in the neck, one can assume that something has gone wrong. The challenge is in knowing what the problem is. That's where the knowledge of biochemistry and all the laboratory tests come in. We needed to know what the normal values are in order to understand the abnormal. They drilled us to death with this biochemistry.

There was a lot of material to absorb and understand. I thought of my organic chemistry teacher back at Hamline University. He would have been helpful at times like this. I had to get through it somehow.

The African herbalists and doctors who took care of me and many others when I was young also understood when something was wrong. They didn't do any lab tests as far as I know. However, sometimes they threw bones onto a mat on the floor. Then they read the alignment and other things in these bones to determine what was ailing you. It is hard to even begin to draw any similarities between this act and a CAT scan or an MRI. However, these people were able to prescribe a concoction of herbs, roots, leaves, and maybe a tail of some animal to cure the disease. Amazingly, some of us are alive today thanks to these medicine men.

I was in my twenties when I started using Western doctors regularly. I believe that buried somewhere in herbalist concoctions is an active ingredient of some medicine that works to cure disease. The challenge is to analyze these mixtures and come up with the active ingredient.

Whether the derangement in a body's function is found by doing lab tests or by throwing bones on the floor, some medicine is generally prescribed to fix the problem. This is where the knowledge of pharmacology comes in. The number of drugs that go on and off the shelves of pharmacies around the world is unbelievable. The amount of money spent on research and development of drugs is beyond comprehension, all of which bears testimony to the complexity of the human body and the environment in which it exists. The chemical structures of the drugs used to cure diseases are generally complicated. The mechanisms by which they work are equally complicated. Some, like antibiotics, attack their enemy at the root of their structure, the DNA or RNA. Others work to improve the normal physiological function of the body such as muscle strength. Whatever the mechanism is, our challenge in pharmacology was to learn the chemistry, mechanism of action, and application of the old and new drugs. This was a tall order indeed. Pharmacology was just as difficult as it was interesting.

Slowly we moved closer to the application of all this knowledge. We had learned the anatomy, the physiology, the pathology, and pharmacology. But we had not seen any live patients yet. We began to learn more about actual diseases such as high blood pressure and kidney disease.

But wait—not all diseases are caused by germs. Some disorders are inherited. So we had to go and learn genetics, the study of genes passed on from parents to their offspring. When put in perspective, genetics becomes fascinating. Even though very few people have actually ever seen those tricky little lines called genes, everybody has seen their manifestations in the likeness of family members. Grandparents always know and say so-and-so looks like their great-grandfather or aunt. But diseases can be passed on as well. They can be inherited by children from their parents, or they can skip a generation.

Genetics can also play tricks on all species. I recently read the story of a woman who was born to a white couple in South Africa. She was much darker than her parents and her siblings. This woman was expelled from the white school that she attended as a child because of the color of her skin. Her parents went so far as to have blood tests done to prove that this was indeed their child. The cruel system of apartheid would not let her stay in an all-white school because genetics had thrown a curve ball down her way.

Genetics has taken giant steps in research over the past decades. It is no longer just a study of genes and inheritance, but now includes genetic engineering. If genes that transmit disorders from generation to generation can be identified and altered, perhaps those disorders can be eliminated. That would be a little step for a gene but a giant step for mankind. Medicines that work at the gene level may be developed to fight such diseases as cancer. This would be a wonderful development which would improve the lives of millions of people around the world.

While all this genetic engineering stuff is good news, there is great concern that it can fall into the wrong hands. It is hard to imagine what the architects of apartheid in South Africa would have done if they had such powerful technology at their disposal. Who can imagine what Hitler would have done if he knew about genetic engineering?

One can only hope that good will prevail over evil. We can eliminate such diseases as sickle cell disease, Tay-Sachs disease, and many others.

When I started school at Einstein they were just completing a large auditorium that we later used as our classroom. It had a big stage that could be used for some practical demonstrations. On the day that we learned about blood pressure, the lecturer used this stage effectively. He set up a blood pressure machine with a large-print digital readout. The mercury was visible from every angle of the auditorium. One of the male students was asked to sit down and have his blood pressure taken. He was then hooked up to the machine so that there would be continuous readings throughout the class period.

Somewhere from back stage or side door came a lovely, sexy woman. She just strolled across the stage in front of this poor fellow student. As the rest of the class broke out in laughter, the mercury shot straight up. The lady did not even have to say anything. That was our lesson in the effect of human blood pressure on our emotional state. The point was to demonstrate how labile blood pressure measurements can be. It is therefore important to have several readings taken before concluding that someone has high blood pressure, unless the readings are obviously way out of the normal range.

A similar demonstration was used by another lecturer when she taught us about depression. She introduced the topic and simply carried on lecturing as if nothing was going to happen. Then suddenly a charming, elegantly dressed woman came on stage. She greeted the lecturer and everybody in such a way that one could not be upset about the interruption. Then she continued to talk non-stop. The woman was just so bubbly and elegant that she captivated everybody's attention. After her stunning performance she left the stage. If this had not been a staged event I think the lecturer would have completely lost her train of thought.

But she resumed her lecture without too much trouble. Before the period was over, the same woman appeared on stage. This time she walked slowly, her head was down, her shoulders were somewhat stooped, and her face was droopy. She looked like someone in trouble with the world. The lecturer felt sorry for her and she interrupted her lecture to speak to this pitiful woman. For a moment there was complete silence in the classroom. After a few minutes the lecturer came back to define the different types of depression demonstrated by this woman.

In the manic state someone is over-elated and hyperactive. In the depressed state a person suffers from a depressed mood and slowing down of activity. Our visitor had clearly demonstrated both states.

As our classes became progressively interesting, we itched to get out and see real patients. But the college was not ready to turn us loose yet. We were still a great danger to the people of the Bronx and Westchester. We had learned the basic sciences. We had even learned pharmacology. But we had not learned how to apply these basic principles to real people. We had seen the depressed woman. Now we wanted to know how to get her out of her depression.

The lectures began to focus more on treatment of specific disorders. We could finally apply our knowledge of pharmacology and other subjects.

In the meantime I had adjusted to the life on campus. I had made it so far with very little money. I was entirely dependent on a very small loan from the college. As long as I had enough to eat and enough to buy my school supplies I was alright. I told myself that this was not going to be forever. A year had gone by already. Other students shared my plight. There were students from Kenya, Nigeria, and the Caribbean who also lived in the dormitory. We generally walked together to Van Etten for our meals. But there was one guy who liked an extra sandwich for a snack later on at night. So on the way back from the hospital he always insisted on stopping at Jack's Deli for what he called "Jack's dirty sandwich." Jack's Deli was not the cleanest place in the world. There were cats milling around inside the deli, which always turned me off. But Jack was an amiable fellow. We got to know him well. His deli was the only place within a reasonable walking distance where we could buy little snacks and other things. Toward the end of my stay at Einstein they opened a McDonalds at the Westchester Square. This was a rather long walk away from the dorm. Besides, the prices were much higher than at Jack's Deli.

There was not much of any social life for us on campus. It was not like other college campuses where you have a lot of young people who prefer partying to studying. Here the few of us, particularly the minority students, simply buried our heads in the books. First of all, there was only a handful of us, about six or seven out of 177 students in my class. Second, most of us were much older than the average student. We had come to medical school via other careers or a tortuous route like mine. Some had been nurses; others had been teachers. And still others had worked in biotech jobs. As a result we viewed being at Einstein as a once-in-a-lifetime opportunity that was not to be wasted.

There was a bar right next to Jack's Deli called the Tundra. I don't believe any of us ever visited the bar even for one drink. Those were days of social drought in the Tundra region. Our focus was on the top of the mountain. One way or the other we were going to get there.

Under normal circumstances I would have had lots of fun and parties to attend while I was at Einstein. My friends John and Richard always invited me to receptions and parties at the United Nations. There were lots of these parties in those days. I always turned them down. Instead I would head to the library. Mrs. Gardner was the librarian who used to be on duty in the evenings and on weekends. She was a lovely old lady who knew where to find virtually everything in the library. I got to know her well. She even invited me for dinner at her house once. I guess she felt sorry for me because I was always in the library.

There was a nursing school near Van Etten Hospital. Again, under normal circumstances this would have been fertile ground for social life. Instead it was like green grass viewed from atop a camel's hump in the Sahara Desert. I just told myself that there was honey at the top of the mountain. And so I kept on climbing.

When the college felt that we had covered the basic science of the human body from head to toe they were almost ready to turn us loose. Arrangements were made for us to buy our white coats. These were the short white jackets that distinguished us from the attending physicians, who wore the long coats. We also bought our black medicine bags. We were like little kids. I was thrilled to death. If someone didn't know, they would think that I had obtained my MD degree already. But for me this was the highest level that I had ever reached in my quest for a degree in medicine. It was the most visible symbol of progress toward my goal. I had my own stethoscope and my own sphygmomanometer—a big word for a blood pressure machine. It reminded me of the big word—enthusiasm—that I had learned when I was in Standard 4.

In the black bag there was also a reflex hammer and a tourniquet to use when drawing blood. We tried everything except actually drawing blood because that hurt. Otherwise when the first day of clinical rotations came, we were ready.

The whole curriculum was structured in such a way that each phase used the knowledge obtained from the one before. The first thing that we learned was the basic science. This gave us the foundation upon which the practice of medicine is based. Then we had clinical rotations, which gave us a glimpse of what each discipline was all about. Then we had the opportunity to do electives in areas of our interest. The assumption was that by then we had an idea of what we wanted to do upon graduating from medical school. For the most part this was an excellent layout that allowed all the pieces to fall in place.

However, my own wish would have been to go back to the classroom for a while after clinical rotations. This would allow the students to put into perspective what they learned in the basic sciences.

Armed with our black bags and white jackets, we left the classroom. From now on the hospital wards would be our classrooms. We scattered in every direction. The clinical rotations covered such areas as medicine, pediatrics, surgery, obstetrics and gynecology, and psychiatry. It must have been almost a nightmare for the person in charge of organizing the assignments. Everybody rotated through all the departments at some point in time. But, of course, we did different things at different hospitals.

For example, I did psychiatry and surgery at Bronx Lebanon Hospital and did obstetrics and gynecology at Lincoln Hospital. Each hospital had its strengths and weakness. In some cases it was the people who taught you that made the difference. In others, it was the patients that you dealt with that influenced the quality of your experience. Whatever it was, we all had stories to tell about each rotation. Those experiences influenced our career choices.

My rotations in pediatrics at Montefiore Hospital and Morissania Hospital were the most beautiful experiences. The people that I was assigned to were just super. The teaching was excellent. The staff was very friendly. Sometimes these clinical rotations were a very humbling and frustrating experience. In those places where the staff treated you like you knew nothing, it was hard to enjoy the rotation. It was even worse when the patients treated you the same way. Some patients did not hesitate to tell you to get them a real doctor. Such treatment was not easy to accept. It deflated that balloon that we were flying as medical students playing doctor.

But realizing that this was part of that transformation in progress made it easy to swallow. The whole transformation process was designed to enable us to deal with a whole range of personalities. When people are not feeling well or when their loved ones are not well, they tend to be hypersensitive. Physicians need to develop the sensitivity that enables them to deal with these changing emotions. Every physician will have their patience tried to the limit on more than one occasion in their career.

One of the most common assignments that medical students get is to take the history from patients. This is actually a wonderful learning experience. It teaches students how to approach and talk to patients. It teaches them how to listen to the whole story and not rush to conclusions. More importantly, it teaches them about the evolution of the disease or illness and the minor signs and symptoms that the patient may have missed but become important clues to the diagnosis.

A well-written history starts at the beginning of the illness and includes all the signs and symptoms experienced along the way. While this may be excellent for the student, it is oftentimes murder to the patient. They have to sit there and patiently relate this whole story which they have done a thousand times before. In the meantime, they may be in pain or be suffering from whatever ails them. No wonder some of them say, "Get me a real doctor."

Depending upon the hospital and the resident that you were assigned to, you got to do a lot or very little. When I did internal medicine I got to do a lot. I still recall one patient that I was almost exclusively assigned to. He was in the hospital the whole time that I was there. Mr. Holland was an elderly gentleman suffering from cancer. He was losing his memory. However, he managed to surprise us on many occasions. There was this routine where during rounds we asked him what day it was or what month it was. Somehow even when I had seen him earlier and noticed that he was confused, he got the answers correct when we made rounds. This made me look bad. It took a while to realize that when the nurses made their rounds just before us, they told him what day or month it was. And of course he remembered this when we came along shortly after they left.

It was very hard to get blood from this man. He had been stuck everywhere. I got to know where to go in order to draw blood from him.

One of the most difficult things to do as a medical student is to overcome the fear of doing or saying something wrong to a patient. Sometimes that fear or anxiety can interfere with the way that student performs. It's worse when the patient is hostile or intimidating. On one occasion I was asked to take the history from a patient that was described as a VIP. But I did not know how this patient came to be a VIP.

I nervously introduced myself and smiled sheepishly before I got enough courage to ask questions clearly. I was surprised that she answered my questions so clearly that she virtually wrote the history for me. She turned out to be a famous radiologist that had written the books that we were reading for radiology. She had a chest X-ray done. We asked her to read her own X-ray. This patient was not just another patient or doctor; she was also a teacher. She knew that I was a nervous medical student, and so she wanted to ease my anxiety and teach me a few things along the way. I appreciated that.

We had already spent many months learning basic science. We had learned a lot of pharmacology. Now we were trying to relate those drugs to the diseases that they were designed to treat. In the process, we had to learn about the side effects of these drugs in different people and different age groups. This is one of the most important distinctions that one needs to understand in pediatrics. Proper doses are critical in children because mistakes can easily cause harm.

We also had to learn a new language of sorts. The symbols and abbreviations used in writing prescriptions had always looked like just scribbles to me. I had to learn what bid, tid, and so on mean. I finally found an area where all those years of studying Latin paid off. These abbreviations made more sense when I recalled the Latin words from which they came.

We had all learned how to tell stories as children. Now we were learning how to tell these stories in medical terms. The history that we took from patients was presented to the other doctors on rounds. It was helpful to be a good storyteller because then the only thing you had to worry about was being able to use the proper medical terminology.

We had a lot of opportunities to practice this part of the art.

A lot of things had eased up a little bit by now. The intensity of basic science courses was over. My fear and anxiety about medical school had vanished, and my financial situation had changed slightly. In the last two years of medical school, I got a partial tuition scholarship from the United Nations. I will forever be grateful to the late George Silundika for helping me with the application. He was a good man.

I also had a little more time to do some work. Since I had learned how to draw blood, I did this to make a few dollars—ten dollars a day whenever I worked. I used to get up early in the morning and go to Jacobi Hospital to draw blood on patients on the various wards. Most of the patients were on the surgical floors.

I will never forget one patient who had sustained burn wounds over most of his body. To me it looked like there was no part of the body left intact. Going to draw blood from him was the most agonizing experience. But he was such a gentleman that even if you missed the first time he would let you try a different site. Those were the days when I would go to my room and thank God for everything that he had given me. This man was in so much pain that I literally felt his pain, too.

The rest of my day was still spent on clinical rotations. At about the same time that I worked at Jacobi Hospital I was doing a rotation in psychiatry at the Bronx Lebanon Hospital. This was an interesting experience for me. I had never really convinced myself that psychiatry belongs in medicine.

This was really a reflection of my background. When I was growing up I never heard of a doctor treating mental illness. I was under the impression that people with mental illnesses were simply locked up somewhere. There was a place in my hometown called *Ingutsheni*. This was a psychiatric hospital. However, I had never been there. The way in which people talked about it was as if patients were simply kept there for protection.

My first encounter with a psychiatric patient was in a maternity ward. The doctor that we were working with had been asked to see a patient that had just delivered a baby a couple of days earlier. She had become withdrawn and was tearful. She had refused to take care of herself. She would not eat or take a bath. The attending physician took us with him to see this patient. He tried everything that he knew. This woman would not say a word. He finally recommended inpatient psychiatric care for her.

I saw her every day for about a week. She took the medication that she was given. I was pleased to see her open up and return to her normal self. I thought that was remarkable, and I learned to respect psychiatry as a great discipline in the field of medicine.

I felt a great sense of relief at the completion of all the basic clinical rotations. My feeling was that now very little could stand in the way to prevent me from graduating. However, we still had to take several electives and one extended rotation in a discipline of our choice. This was generally the area that you would ultimately do your residency in. I had made up my mind that pediatrics would be my field of choice. I did a number of other electives including radiology, community medicine, nephrology, cardiology and pathology, which turned out to be very interesting.

I still winced when I saw a dead body and could not get myself to be comfortable cutting into a human being. But the course was led by Dr. Angrist, a world-renowned pathologist. He was a remarkable old man who was able to take what appeared to be a gruesome site and make it into an incredible learning experience. By the end of the day I found myself so involved with the procedures and analysis that I forgot all about how grisly the original site was.

Dr. Angrist would explain why he felt the bullet went in here, missed this organ, and came out there. He would look at the liver and give you ten things that could make it look the way it did. He was just a phenomenal teacher.

The elective in community medicine was useful to me. I learned all about the different types of hospitals, the city or public hospitals, the voluntary hospitals, and proprietary hospitals. I learned about the populations where the various hospitals were located. We did analyses of neighborhoods in terms of socioeconomic status, language, and prevalence of different diseases. We also learned about different types of health care systems and tried to find the strengths and weaknesses of each. The whole idea was to be able to see patients as whole individuals and not just their diseases. That way it would be possible to understand and perhaps prevent recurring hospitalizations or visits to the emergency room.

A good example would be a child who has asthma and lives in a roach-infested project. No matter how many times you treat this child, chances are that he or she will keep coming back until the home environment is corrected.

Finally, I did my extended clinical rotation, or sub-internship, in pediatrics at the Bronx Lebanon Hospital. It was a great learning experience. They treated us like interns. For all practical purposes we were interns because we were just a few months shy of graduating. We each had our own panel of patients that we were expected to know everything about. We did night calls just like the interns and residents. This was real stuff. We were now almost real doctors. The only thing left was to get that sheepskin.

I saw many interesting cases. Our chief of service was Dr. Murray Davidson, who was a pediatric gastroenterologist. We got many cases that were referred to him for evaluation. I had the opportunity to work with him on some of his patients. I saw patients with ulcerative colitis, Crohn's disease, and Gaucher's disease. He was a highly meticulous and disciplined clinician. Everything had to be done very well. Otherwise, when he roared at rounds, everybody felt like running for cover.

I had the opportunity to work in the emergency room during my sub-internship. At first this was a rather scary place to be. A lot of the anxiety had to do with the fact that it is always the case that no one can predict what will come through the doors. However, after a while I realized that it was a place where the unexpected is almost the norm.

One day a young woman brought a baby. She sat in the waiting room with everybody for a while. Then she asked somebody to hold the baby for her for a minute. This other person thought the young lady had gone to the bathroom or something. After holding the baby for what seemed an unusually long time, she began to look for the mother. The young lady was nowhere to be found. When the nurses looked in the bag that the mother had brought, they discovered a big surprise. The mother had written a note which asked that someone else take care of the baby. In the note she did not elaborate except to say that she could not take care of the baby. This was a very clean, well-dressed baby. She was wrapped in a clean pink blanket. There was food for the baby in the bag. I was dumbfounded and numbed by what had happened. I could not imagine what would drive a mother to abandon her baby like that. I never found out what happened to the baby or if the mother was ever found. For me that was just a glimpse at the side of medicine that is not taught in any textbook. I have since seen more bizarre situations.

At the conclusion of my sub-internship I had reached the top of the mountain. The only thing left was for me to receive a flag with my name and the letters MD inscribed on it. I would plant this flag right at the peak of the mountain and proclaim "victory at last."

For me this was an accomplishment not unlike that of Sir Edmund P. Hillary and Tenzing Norgay. They struggled to the top of Mount Everest, and in 1953 they stood at the top of the highest mountain in the world. And I had reached the highest mountain in my own world.

# Chapter 13

# The Moment of Glory

⬡ ⬡ ⬡ ⬡ ⬡ ⬡

To say I was ecstatic is an understatement. I had dreamed of the day when I would get to this point for twenty years. Thursday, June 2, 1977, was the day when I wore the cap and gown and received my diploma as a doctor of medicine. I was thrilled to the bone because I had finally made it to the top of the mountain.

The trail had taken me to many dead ends. I had followed it to many dark alleys where I thought I would never find my way out again. However, each time I was able to turn around or overcome the hurdles and carry on. There were many times when I was downright discouraged. But somehow I always found the strength to bounce back and keep on climbing. I felt like I had established the truth to the expression "Where there is a will there is a way."

About nine years earlier I had reached what was probably my lowest emotional state when I was at the refugee camp in Botswana. From the dungeon of deep despair I wrote a letter to Louise and told her that where my intelligence failed me my determination would carry me through. There had been many times along the way when my intelligence failed me. But each time I told myself that it gets dark sometimes and yet the sun rises again. There was no doubt at this point in time that the sun was up. I was right at the top of the mountain. Everything around me was as bright as it could be.

The dark days at Fletcher High, when Ian Smith declared the Unilateral Declaration of Independences of Rhodesia, which could have derailed my education, were barely visible. The turbulent days at the University of Rhodesia were like dark shadows at the bottom of the mountain. And the dog days at the refugee camp were nothing but bad memories. I was finally going to wear that white coat as a full-fledged doctor like my sister wore her nurse's uniform with pride. I was sad only because my father would not be there to visit me like he visited my sister at Mpilo Hospital twenty years earlier.

The last few months at Albert Einstein were a busy time for me. I was getting ready to leave the little room that had been home to me for four years. I had applied for a residency program in pediatrics in New York. I got into a program that allowed me to rotate between Jacobi Hospital, Albert Einstein College Hospital, and Bronx Lebanon Hospital. I shared the program with a fellow classmate. When she was in the Jacobi Einstein complex, I would be at Bronx Lebanon hospital. Then we would switch places according to the schedule. At the end of the year I was looking forward to this program. So there was no uncertainty about where I was going to be.

Something else had happened along the way to brighten my path. All the stars seemed to have been shining on me. I had met a lovely lady, the woman of my dreams, right in midtown Manhattan, on a bright Saturday afternoon. I had gone there to attend a political meeting addressed by one of our leaders. She happened to be there, too. I had never seen or heard about her before, but it turned out that she was born and raised about fourteen miles from where I was. Our paths had crossed, but we had never seen each other.

She left home to go to school in England long before I left home. I came to the United States via England while she was a student there. Then she came to New York while I was a student in Minnesota. Under the guidance of the stars above, I came to New York to study. And there we met. We have been together since. So as I prepared to graduate from medical school, I was also preparing to get married.

I would have invited the whole world to my graduation if I could. I wrote many letters to tell my friends and family about it. I invited as many people as I could who had been instrumental in my success. My parents, of course, would top that list. I would have loved to have them come for the graduation and wedding. But of course that did not happen for many reasons. My father had passed away in 1970. He had been a powerful and influential figure in my life. For financial and political reasons I was not able to bring my mother over. The country was still in the grips of a serious war for independence from Great Britain. The movement of African people was severely restricted. It had been nearly ten years since I left home, and I had not seen my mother in all those years.

My sister Grace and her husband Ronald had enabled me to get to the US. However, they had gone back to Africa and were working in Zambia at the time. Coming to New York would not have been easy for them. They played such an important role in my success that I can never forget what they did for me. It was my sister Grace who created the spark in my brain to study for a career in medicine. It was she and her husband that made it possible for me to get out of the refugee camp in Botswana and come to the United States. And it was they who enabled me to start school at Hamline University when I was penniless. How could I ever forget them? I would have loved to have them at the ceremonies. They were not able to attend.

Then there was my pen pal Louise Platt. When the stars were shinning on me and lighting my path I could not help but think of her. Our friendship had started as pen pals almost ten years earlier. Louise and her parents turned out to be incredibly beautiful human beings. Our friendship was without any doubt crucial to my success. Louise was instrumental in getting me from Botswana to Minnesota. She organized and paid for my accommodation. She helped me to get some money to start school at Hamline University. I sometimes sit and wonder where I would have gone if she had not come into my world. It's entirely possible that I would have joined the guerilla army somewhere to fight for the liberation of my country. No one knows what could have happened. But that was not to be my destiny. I am grateful that Louise was there at the right time. I will forever be indebted to her. She was able to attend the graduation ceremony.

Leon and Ginny Knight came from St. Cloud, Minnesota, a place that I had never heard of before. I don't know where I would have found that I-20 Form, or how long it would have taken me to get it. But Leon heard my plea and answered the call. Mr. Edgar Whitehead, a former prime minister of Rhodesia, thought he was getting rid of a troublemaker when he deported Mr. Knight. He did not know that it was my stars simply paving the way for me to get out of Rhodesia. The Knights were instrumental in enabling me to get a visa to come to the United States. They will always have a special place in my heart. Unfortunately, they were not able to attend the ceremonies.

The man who guided me through those intense four years at Hamline University was an amazing human being. I will never forget Dr. Olaf Runquist. His energy, his personality, and his intellect were contagious. If there ever was someone born to be a teacher, this was the man. At times, whenever I was feeling low and discouraged, just listening to him and watching him go about his business was enough to get me going. There was never a day when I saw him slow down. He took me under his wings even before I started school at Hamline University. He guided me through the maze of the American education system to a degree in chemistry and biology. And he didn't stop there. He prodded me to apply to medical school even when I doubted my chances. Dr. Runquist was the greatest. When the going was rough in medical school, I always thought of his boundless energy, and it helped me get through the day. I thank him for believing in me. He was not able to attend the ceremonies.

Dr. Wesley St. John, our foreign-students advisor, was great. He was not only there to guide and advise us; he also made us feel at home. His house was our home away from home. May he rest in peace.

There are so many people that made this jigsaw puzzle of my life fit together that, I cannot mention everybody by name. I will always be grateful to all of them for the part they played regardless of how small or big it may have been. They made me who I am today. Without them my *struggle to the top of the mountain* would not have been possible.

# About the Author

* * * * * *

Ernest Simela is a pediatrician who was born in a rural area of Zimbabwe, southern Africa. He graduated from Hamline University in Minnesota and got his doctor of medicine degree from Albert Einstein College of Medicine in New York. He is married, has two sons, and lives and practices in New York.

# About the Book

* * * * * *

This is an inspiring story of courage, hard work, determination, focus, and results. A black little boy born in a remote village of racially segregated Southern Rhodesia (now Zimbabwe), Africa, dreams of one day being a medical doctor.

In a letter to a pen pal 1968 he writes:

"Where my intelligence fails me, my determination will carry me through."

With not a penny to his name, but a pocketful of hopes and dreams, he lands in the United States of America. And then ...

# Endorsements

◈   ◈   ◈   ◈   ◈   ◈

Dr. Ernest Simela recounts how obstacles were placed in his path to making something out of his life. He fought them all, using every tool available. From primary school he aspired to be a medical doctor but colonial Zimbabwe limited his chances to achieve his dream. He would not be deterred though. He vividly describes how he struggled until forced to leave the country of his birth under horrid conditions, including life in a refugee camp and jail. His story is a primary source of information for those who want to learn about what it took to survive and triumph under difficult conditions, in a country transitioning from colonial rule.

Yet there is more to this inspiring story. Dr. Simela chose a path and succeeded because he had role models in his early life: hard working parents who gave him a "can do" streak; a sister whose example he emulated and a teacher who "triggered" something in him. Even as he claims to have "never looked back", he has looked back for us, to what it takes to reach the mountain top. Whatever our backgrounds or cultures, we can all learn from the story of his example.

Handel Njabulo Mlilo, Ph.D.
Strategic Communications Specialist

Ernest Simela has no doubt, succeeded in rekindling memories of most African students, caught in the liberation whirlwind of change that swept over colonial Africa.

"Struggle to the Top of the Mountain," is "His-Story", "My – Story," and "Her-Story "told in a beautiful, elegant, animated, inspiring and nostalgic manner. The narratives of the experiences are by no means identical, but it is safe to say that their genesis are similar. It is the HOPE for a brighter future; driven by ambition, burning desire, and unquenchable determination to lift one's self from deplorable socio-economic conditions of the time. And in turn, offers one's self as Role model for others.

The road was often frosted with seemingly insurmountable difficulties but always; somehow, somewhere a Good Samaritan offered a lifeline to pull you through.

That great Country called the Good Old USofA was and is full of them. Their adage is, "If you work hard, play by the rules, and persevere, you can get to the TOP OF THE MOUNTAIN.

Max Glover.
Retired NYC Sch. Principal